I May Have Pushed Your Buttons,
But I Didn't Install Them

52 Pieces of Practical Wisdom

to Live and Love Effectively

Jennifer Swantkowski, PhD

I May Have Pushed Your Buttons, But I Didn't Install Them
Copyright © 2024 by Jennifer Swantkowski, PhD.

ISBN: 979-8-9860523-1-1

First edition.

Author website: www.jenniferswanphd.com

Disclaimer:

The information in this book is meant for educational and informational purposes only. It is not intended to serve directly or indirectly as a substitute for clinical, therapeutic, or medical advice or intervention.

Clinical vignettes are amalgamations of actual client interactions the author has experienced over the past thirty years. Details have been changed to protect their anonymity. Best efforts have been taken to attribute terms, quotes, and phrases to the appropriate original source when possible.

For Dan, my friend and editor,
none of this would have been possible without you!

For Sandra, my friend, mentor,
life raft, and sounding board.

For Mom and Dad,
my eternal role models. I love you.

For my fiercely loyal and loving family,
you are my heart with arms and legs.

Contents

And So, It Begins...

Over the past twenty-eight years, I have worked with thousands of clients representing all ages, all socioeconomic spheres, various ethnicities, cultural backgrounds, religious affiliations, genders, and sexual orientations. I have found there are a few key truths that exist across and through these various realms of human experience: 1) In the words of Harry Stack Sullivan, "We are all more human than otherwise." 2) We all have five core needs from the cradle to the grave: to be seen, heard, held, valued, and understood. 3) As we seek to receive and serve others in the fulfillment of these core needs, we often miss the forest for the trees and spend our lives in a semi-frustrated state, and as Thoreau stated, "living lives of quiet desperation," waiting for someone to come and save us. Spoiler alert: No one is coming; that part is up to us.

We may get highly creative in developing complex defenses to *protect* us when these core needs aren't met. However, I have yet to work with an individual, a couple, or a family where these five core needs and the degree to which they were being fulfilled were not integral to their story and reason for seeking my services.

As children, we rely on our families, teachers, and others to address these core needs. As we get older, we often learn the hard way that it is only through the ongoing practice of honing our relational skills, strategies, and mindset that we can offer and receive the meeting of these needs to truly live and love effectively.

Unfortunately, today's modern world is operating at a speed not optimal for wisdom to catch up, let alone stick around. As a result, we find ourselves feeling more lonely, invisible, disconnected, anxious, agitated, fragmented, and isolated than ever before. We have replaced personal responsibility with blame and projection. So many of us are hungrier than ever to be seen, heard, held, valued, and understood. Yet, we tend to hide behind memes, avatars, and social media facades that only show our best "beach vacation" selves and opt to *block* or *cancel* anything that threatens our fragile sense of reality and self. However, all it takes is a few courageous humans to lead with authenticity, humility, and a desire to seek commonality rather than difference, to shine the light for others to join the march back to health and the full range of our humanity.

I May Have Pushed Your Buttons, But I Didn't Install Them is a collection of a few pearls of practical wisdom that I have gathered throughout my life and career. It consists of sensible accountability practices and strategies for generating emotional resilience and relational freedom. Resilience and freedom come with the realization that not only do we all have these core needs, but we are ultimately responsible for cultivating an environment in which we can offer them to ourselves and others. I hope you enjoy reading the pages that follow and that a few of these pearls might be useful as you string together your own necklace of tools, skills, strategies, goals, and ideals.

"Triggered" Is Not an Emotion

I am not sure when this word not only invaded our language but stepped in as a vernacular grenade with the power to shut people down. All that has to be said these days is, "You are triggering me," and suddenly, the onus is shifted to the other person not only for causing the discomfort that we are experiencing but to stop making us feel uncomfortable or distressed. Being "triggered" typically refers to a series of reactions that occur in our emotional and physical beings that make us aware that we are feeling unsafe, overwhelmed, upset, or typically some other negative emotional or physical response.

While it is more than okay to have limits to what behaviors and/or language we choose to put up with from others in our lives, it is our responsibility to understand our reactions so we can have agency over our response, and then thoughtfully set appropriate limits. One thing that I have found helpful at times is the powerful reminder. *Well, they may have pushed my buttons, but they didn't install them.* This shifts the responsibility back to me to better understand my own emotional Achilles' heels. I can then choose to either deal with "my stuff" by myself or let the people in my life that I care about know what I'm grappling with while keeping in mind that it is most likely not their intention to hurt me.

This perpetuates personal responsibility as well as the awareness that it is not the job of others to know us as well or better than we know ourselves, nor is it their responsibility to take care of us. Not everything is about us, even if it affects us. Even people who love us and are in our "inner circle" are going to mess up sometimes and say the wrong thing at the wrong time. We get to choose to not be *so* on guard and reactive and to practice a little tolerance and acceptance. Now certainly, if we've made it clear that there are ways of being treated or words and actions that are hurtful to us, and our loved ones or friends continue to go right for the jugular, then that is a different issue. In that case, saying we feel "triggered" is still probably not the most effective thing to do. Recognizing what we are feeling—not valued, misunderstood, alone, etc.—and communicating those feelings directly will typically be more effective in yielding our desired outcome.

In terms of the world at large and people not in our inner sanctum, they are not here on this planet to *not trigger* us. We are most likely not even on their radar screens. They are doing their own thing. And again, truly little is about us as individuals, even if it directly affects us. We are moving too far away from personal responsibility these days, and as a result, we are feeling increasingly victimized. If we go looking for something, there's a good chance we will find it. If we are fairness junkies, we will locate a lot of inequities. But if we search for perfectly imperfect yet well-meaning people, we will find a lot of that as well. If I am an orange and someone squeezes me, lemon juice doesn't come out. When I get squeezed—or triggered by life—Jen juice comes out, not Mom or Dad juice, not my boss's juice, or my next-door neighbor's juice. It is then up to me to look at my "Jen juice" and decide if I like what is coming out of me or not. I get to decide if I need to ask for some space, draw a limit, hold a boundary, and/or if I need to slow down and realize that this is *my* "juice" and something I need to better understand and work on. I can then decide if I like how I am feeling and reacting, with the knowledge that I don't have to let anyone, anything, or any circumstance co-opt my own personal agency and my choice in how I respond.

A dear friend called me one night and was talking about how she felt she was being passive-aggressive and sometimes just downright mean to her husband. She had all sorts of justifiable reasons to be angry and hurt. For years, she felt left alone to navigate the major events in their lives. Now, even when he tried and showed up in small ways, she found herself unable to appreciate it as he continued to fail her in ways that she felt were most important. By the end of our call, she had realized that she had a right to be angry, hurt, and frustrated. But she had given up her agency and was now a walking reaction to what he said and did. She valued being a kind, fair, warm, and patient person. Now she felt bitter and cold and was constantly scanning, primed, and ready for the next injustice. In doing so, she didn't feel stronger or more empowered; she felt angrier and more "triggered." Ultimately, she would have to decide if she could remain married and if they could find a working middle ground. However, in the meantime, she could focus on her own side of the street, tend to her own leaking juice, and show up in a manner conducive to her own values, regardless of his actions and behavior.

Nobody owes us anything. This is a cold hard truth. Most of the world and the people in it are not walking around holding us in mind. This is not because they are bad, uncaring people. It's because our "stuff" is not at the forefront of other people's minds. Everyone is in their own hula hoop just trying to manage their own complicated life. Again, most things aren't personal. Even things our own loved ones say and do are typically not about us, despite affecting us. When evidence shows the contrary, by all means, we should speak to our experience and set limits for ourselves. Otherwise, it is best to understand what it means to be "triggered" and then focus first on the things that are within our control. Namely, on our own "juice." We can then choose (or not) to speak to our actual feelings rather than react with urgency and weaponize our language with words like "triggered," expecting others to not only understand us but to work to change their behavior for our comfort.

Scarcity Versus Abundance

A favorite quote of mine, by Anais Nin, that my clients hear me say over and over again is the reminder, "We don't see the world as it is; we see the world as we are." If the lens by which we view and engage the world is one of scarcity, we will often feel diminished and victimized and will only notice what is lost or absent versus what is available and possible. It is important to note that if we are looking for something, there is a much greater likelihood of finding it. If we are looking for all the ways in which our partner or spouse does not meet our needs, guess what we are going to locate more often than not? Exactly! All the places they have come up short.

Alternatively, suppose the lens by which we view our relationship is one of abundance. In that case, we are much more likely to notice the times our spouse/partner makes the effort to see, meet, and get us, along with the other virtues they bring to the relationship.

Scarcity and abundance mindsets do not have much to do with material things. That is one realm in which the reality of scarcity or abundance shows up; however, even there, it is more the attitude with which we perceive our material possessions that determines our perspective than the items themselves. My grandma grew up in poverty and spent the early part of her life in abuse, but when I came to know her in her later years, she was the richest person I knew. Not because she had a lot of money, but because she had an abundance of grace. Her home was small, and she did not have a lot of extra money after paying her monthly bills, but I never once heard that woman complain. I never once heard her speak about the misfortunes—and there had been many—in her life. She focused on the gifts that life had granted her and chose to see the world and her space in it as a gift. Later in life, when I learned of all that she had been through, I was even more impressed by how she had decided to maneuver her way in the world.

It's not about what we have or don't have or our circumstances; it's about our response to our circumstances. Some of the richest people I have ever met were during my years of working in hospice with adults and children in the final months or days of their lives. Talk about a justifiable fall into a scarcity mentality when facing such limited time and interrupted opportunity, yet so many found and focused on their gratitude and grace rather than a sense of resentment and bitterness.

Scarcity is born out of fear. It inhibits generosity of the spirit. The fear is that there is not enough to go around. Thus, we will miss out. On the other hand, abundance stems from faith that there is always enough, and if we don't get ours this time around, it's okay; perhaps it was meant to be that way. Abundance allows us to genuinely want the best for other people and cheer on their accomplishments. Scarcity has us silently fist-bumping and feeling delight when someone fails. Abundance is faith and trust in the idea that we are all deserving of our time here on earth. Not one of us earned it; it was granted. We can choose to be teammates or opponents. We can bend to allow someone to use our back to achieve their goal, trusting that someone will be there for us when we need that extra boost. And if that day comes and that boost or help doesn't arrive as we would have hoped or we feel left behind, we recognize that as someone else's scarcity model at work, and we don't have to take it personally.

Often when I am working with couples, I will find that there is a covert or sometimes even overt scorekeeping going on. Scorekeeping is a tactic of scarcity. *I did this for you, and you didn't do that for me. You had two guys' nights; now it's my turn. I did the dishes and cooked all week, what did you do? I spent years standing beside you while you got your advanced degree; what are you going to do for me?* Is this common? Sure. Effective? Nope, not really.

I had one wife ask me, "Why should I work so hard and carry the extra weight while he (her husband) tries this new career?"

My answer was, "Because you can." She could certainly choose not to do so. We are allowed, even as people of abundance, to know our limits and to opt out. Unfortunately, what she chose to do was to pull the extra weight, resentful the whole way through and continuously bringing up the day when she could cash in her chips on all that she felt she was now owed. This is scarcity. Abundance isn't about the other person but about what lives inside us. It is our attitude, and we can either cultivate one driven by fear and measurement or one driven by generosity and allowance.

This is not an invitation for us to place ourselves in a position of being abused or exploited. The offering should not come as a result of a threat or demand. That is a hostage situation, not a relationship. Abundance begins and ends with us. We cannot give what we do not have, and if we are not taking care of ourselves, the well will run dry no matter how much we want to keep giving. So, we must choose wisely and realize we do not have endless psychic energy. We need to slow down and ask ourselves the question, "Am I walking through the world looking for what is wrong, where I am not getting my due, and taking some delight in other people's misfortunes?" If so, we will also find that we are quite miserable and that our conversations are often focused on other people or complaining about our lives.

When I was twenty-eight, my uncle died, leaving three young children to my mom and dad, who were beyond middle age. I no longer have two biological brothers; I have five brothers and sisters. Mom and Dad modeled that with love there is always room at the table. Squeeze in, pick up the slack, reach down and help someone up, share, offer, step up, step closer, offer some more. Why? Because we can.

03 Take Care of Our Own Side of the Street

The idea of taking care of our own side of the street is often heard in the world of addiction recovery. However, it is a powerfully important rule for life in general. Too frequently, we are focused on what someone else is doing or how someone else is showing up, and we use this as a marker and determinant of what we do and how we show up. In doing this, we become nothing more than a walking reaction to the world around us, taking our cues from others and external circumstances rather than having an internal focus and locus of control. Having an internal locus of control means that one believes they are their best tool in the game of life. By looking and relying within, we are aware of our values and focused on living in alignment with them. The person who is taking care of their side of the street is busy doing their work and focused on their own emotional and physical productivity rather than being a fairness junkie and watching and measuring what other people have or do.

Stoicism is an ancient philosophy with a very practical and relevant reach for those interested in how to live effectively in today's world. The four cardinal virtues of Stoicism are temperance, wisdom, courage, and justice. Each of these virtues is evident in the concept of taking care of and staying on one's own side of the street.

To live with temperance is to slow down, maintain self-discipline, and operate in moderation and balance. Instant gratification and excess rarely lead to lasting contentment. When we constantly look at what our neighbors have or do, we are in a world focused on comparison and competition, and it becomes a challenge to remain in a balanced self-state.

Living in the virtue of wisdom means knowing oneself. It means understanding our strengths and vulnerabilities and being mindful of them as we walk through life. Accumulating wisdom is a marathon, not a sprint. It develops over time, with a great deal of reflection and humility, and requires discipline, patience, and commitment.

Living courageously means living in moderation and balance (temperance) and allowing ourselves the time and space to better understand ourselves (wisdom), as we make conscious decisions to be warriors in our own life. Living in courage means recognizing that life isn't guaranteed to be fair or easy, yet we still step into the arena ready to take on whatever challenges life hands us.

The virtue of justice often trips people up. Again, the fairness junkies of the world mistake this to mean that they need to be hypervigilant and call people out on their missteps. While justice does mean using sound judgment to determine what is fair and just in the world, it is also about recognizing our own judgments and biases and doing the challenging work to check ourselves.

Again, this goes back to the idea that if you are an orange and are squeezed, lemon juice doesn't come out. We are responsible for our own "juice." What flavor is yours? Is your juice one of courage, temperance, justice, and wisdom? Or do you get squeezed, and your juice is victimization, anger, resentment, and blame?

If we wake up each day and focus our work on these four virtues in our daily actions, by default, we will have no space or time to gaze over the fence, searching for how others are showing up.

It's never too early to start learning this principle. I have a young niece who is sandwiched between two brothers. Being intelligent, aware, and kind are a few of her greatest assets. Unfortunately, that intelligence and awareness are sometimes misdirected as she can become quite focused on what her brothers are doing or not doing. I have watched many times as the joy in her face is replaced with frustration and annoyance. She puts her own toys down as she feels compelled to make sure that they are being fair, kind, and just. The external focus for this little one, and all of us big kids, can become a hard habit to break and drain the color out of our world very quickly. We can't be in two places at once. We cannot be all up in our friend/partner/neighbor/family member's business and be entirely focused on our work and taking care of our own side of the street.

Author's Note: *To learn more about Stoicism and its practical applications in today's world, check out Ryan Holiday at The Daily Stoic, http://dailystoic.com/*

In the Light of Eternity & Amor Fati

In 2015, Joel Lovell interviewed the popular American co-median and talk show host Stephen Colbert for *Gentlemen's Quarterly* magazine. It's a wonderful interview, but the part that moved me the most was when Colbert was discussing the sudden death of his father and two siblings when he was ten years old. "I was left alone a lot after my dad and the boys died… and it was just me and my mom for a long time… by her example, I was not bitter. By *her* example, she was not bitter. Broken, yes. Bitter, no." He went on to describe that even in her days of unremitting grief, she drew on her faith that the only way not to be swallowed by sorrow is, in fact, to recognize that our sorrow is inseparable from our joy, to always understand our suffering and ourselves, in the light of eternity. "You gotta love the bomb," he said, (a piece of wisdom conveyed to him as an adult by Second City director Jeff Michalski), and "Boy did I have a bomb when I was ten. That was quite an explosion. And I learned to love it. So, that's why... maybe, I don't know. That may be why you don't see me as someone angry and working out my demons onstage. It's that I love the thing that I most wish had not happened." As the interviewer asked for clarification on how you could love the thing you don't want, Colbert shared a story about Tolkien in which a priest had written him a letter questioning his view that death was not a punishment for the fall but a gift. Colbert relays, "Tolkien says, in a letter back: 'What punishments of God are not gifts?'" As his eyes filled with tears, Colbert went on, "So, it would be ungrateful to not take *everything* with gratitude. It doesn't mean you want it. I can hold both of those ideas in my mind... it's not the same thing as wanting it to have happened. But you can't change everything about the world. You certainly can't change things that have already happened."

Both of these points—choosing to see things from the perspective of "in the light of eternity" and deciding to "love the bomb"—are also central ideas seen in ancient Stoic philosophy. We need to take our view from the Cosmos, go high and wide, to see the larger perspective. From here, we can move from a myopic and comparative stance to one that allows us to not take ourselves and everything that happens to us so personally or seriously. If we are able to see our lives in the light of eternity, we realize we are but a speck. If we view death in the light of eternity, it puts all the billions of people that have passed before us in our purview, and we can now view death as the great equalizer. We can see life as the thing we might choose to engage in with a bit more grace and levity as it is something we will never get out of alive. As we choose to "love the bomb," we embrace the all-important concept of Amor Fati. Amor Fati translates to *love your fate.* However, I believe it is more in line with what Colbert has implied: *accept your fate.* Accept that this is what life has delivered. At the conclusion of the interview, Colbert shared something that moved the interviewer to the point of writing it down and carrying it with him wherever he goes: "It's our choice whether to hate something in our lives or to love every moment of them, even the parts that bring us pain. At every moment, we are volunteers."

If we go high and wide and contemplate all that came before us and all that will come after us, we can cease the pull to feel sorry for ourselves or to operate from a mentality of scarcity. If we are open, we can shift our perspective to one in which we view loss, challenges, and circumstances—both good and bad—in the light of eternity and with full acceptance of our fate. When we can do this, we can realize that we are but one chord in the vast symphony of existence and that, as volunteers, we are given a chance to choose in each moment, over and over again, how we will respond to our lives, ourselves, and others.

Slowing Down to the Speed of Wisdom

Have you all seen the funny meme floating around Instagram that says: How to politely tell someone they are stupid: *Wisdom has been chasing you, but you've always been faster!* While I am certainly not calling anyone stupid, there is a lot of truth in the fact that we are often running around like chickens with our heads cut off, eluding the much slower, richer pace of wisdom. The Oxford Dictionary defines wisdom as "The soundness of an action or decision with the application of experience, knowledge, and good judgment."

In the psychological modality of Dialectical Behavioral Therapy, they distinguish between rational mind, emotional mind, and wise mind. A wise mind is seen as one that can rely on the interplay of both the rational and emotional mind and the concept of mindfulness to intentionally respond versus react in any given situation. In my favorite philosophy of Stoicism, wisdom is viewed as the capacity to differentiate between the things we can and cannot control and between what is and isn't truly important in our lives. How do we know what is truly in or out of our control and differentiate if something is really worthy of an investment of our time? By slowing down, tapping into our experience, our knowledge, and the knowledge and experience of others whom we value, then making an intentionally sound decision to respond rather than react.

Unfortunately, several things in today's day and age are getting in the way of our capacity to get into our wise minds. We spend so much of our time thrashing about in the crashing waves and riptides of life that we are unable to see the calmer waters that lay underneath the surface. We must go deeper to reach the stillness. We have to fly above the turbulence to find clearer skies. How do we do this? With intention. It is way too easy for us to get caught up in the 24/7 endless loop of information coming at us. We are held hostage by the algorithms that fool and lull us into a false validation of being known on social media; the constant itch of FOMO (fear of missing out) that comes with the endless, filtered posts of people we hardly know leading unbelievably wonderful lives. Not to mention the deluge of content overload we're met with every time we Google anything.

When I was writing my dissertation, I had to distill down thousands of books, articles, and documents online to figure out what was relevant and essential for my topic. Had I authored that same dissertation thirty years earlier, I would have had to search long and hard, deliberately and with intention, just to find the sources to back up my hypothesis. Thank God for the internet, right? … Yes and no. Technology, with all its gifts, has also created an erosion of some of our capacities. Capacities that are important in strengthening our wise minds, such as our ability to tolerate frustration, our capacity to delay gratification, our ability to use our minds to figure things out and/or give our minds a moment to call up a memory or a piece of information. Now, way too often, the moment we can't remember the name of that band in the 80s we love, we don't take the time to let it come to us. We Google it. What happens when you don't use your mind? Just like any other muscle in your body, it atrophies. We used to order things that took six weeks to get to our doorsteps. Now, we find ourselves frustrated when we can't get what we want from Amazon in 48 hours. Today, if we want to know the best natural home remedy for a sore throat, we don't ask Grandma, who was around before the antibiotic craze; we ask Reddit. Do you know who makes up Reddit? Who the hell knows? That's the point. We turn to Reddit or Quora and gather information from someone who could be a seventeen-year-old crackhead living out of his parent's car for all we know. We want what we want when we want it, and how we want it. And when that doesn't happen—we react.

I am not advocating for ditching technology and living off the grid. There were plenty of people who were not tapping into their wise minds well before the advent of the internet.

So, how do we develop a wise mind? Cultivating wisdom is a choice. It is intentional. It is eyes open, ears listening, and being receptive to what resonates for you as an individual. It is being open to the idea of not always being the expert. It is about realizing you have a limited amount of f*cks to give in this world. It's about taking a beat to let the spaces between the fast flow of information and noise help guide you. Phrases like, *I don't know, let me give that some thought,* or *That's a good point, let me sit with that a minute,* are not only your right but may also lead to better outcomes and less conflict than the drive to ACT NOW.

Be open and courageous enough to differentiate yourself from the highly reactive masses and stand calm in your right to intentionally decide your response and next step. Slow down and let the spirit of wisdom catch you.

"We Are All More Human Than Otherwise."

- Harry Stack Sullivan

I first read this quote well over two decades ago, and it has profoundly shaped and defined my work as a therapist, friend, family member, and fellow human being. At a time when we seem hyper-focused on what divides us, it is imperative that we slow down and scan for our commonalities and places where we can join rather than avoid, separate, dismiss, cancel, or discard.

As we look around, we see that the people here with us have also been granted this particular time slot here on Earth. I didn't earn my time slot, did you? I don't remember experiencing something as a soul that pushed me forward in the queue to arrive here on this planet at this time and granted me a shot at human life.

That is what came to me when I first read Sullivan's quote. Who am I to judge another? Who am I to believe my time here on earth has more importance than anyone else's? Conversely, who am I to believe that my right to be here is less meaningful than anyone else? Who am I to capitulate or show up insecure or in deference to other humans who are simply joining me on this rotation of an earthwalk?

This mindset was acutely influential in developing my psychotherapeutic approach over the years. I began to scan for humanity rather than the potential pathology in my clients. I looked beyond the alphabet soup of mental health diagnoses and focused on the idea that this is an individual in front of me who is grappling with various issues. And what a gift it is that I might be able to walk with and help another one of my fellow travelers.

Instead of judging myself and others as less or more deserving, or bad or good, based on our choices and behavior, I began to find joy and appreciation for all of the distinct roles my earth siblings created with their lives. I was grateful when one had decided to learn how to fix an air conditioner or a car, pick up trash, or fly a plane. All those roles were not only essential to greater humanity but also all deserving of my respect and grace.

While more difficult, we can also choose to accept the challenge and offer grace to those who may have forgotten (or never knew) that they are deserving. These individuals often present poorly, act small or rude, or act out of a puffed-up, insecure place and show up reeking of grandiosity and demanding our respect. Again, while we might be justified in putting them in their place or responding with rudeness in return, imagine if we could lean on Sullivan's sentiment and offer light in their darkness. Or at the very least, not let their darkness become our own.

Being mindful that we are all more human than otherwise has allowed me to forgive and to help my clients see forgiveness as a gift. *Why should I forgive this ass clown who has been nothing but rude to me?* Of course, it's your choice. However, when we are committed to searching for how we are more alike than different, then we can slow down and appreciate that sometimes the human standing in front of us may be doing the best that they can. If they are not showing up well, instead of assuming the worst, we could be open to the possibility that they might be grappling with something that we cannot see or understand. I am not advocating for remaining in an abusive situation or allowing yourself to be walked on by someone. I am talking about the power inherent in allowing another person to show up as themselves at that moment while knowing that we can never really know what is at play in another person's psyche and experience. Through the lens of humility, we can remember our own less-than-perfect moments and the times our own edges and wounds drove us to react or not show up well. In that moment of remembrance, we can choose to offer up the grace we hope that someone has or will show us in one of our less-than-ideal times.

We are all more human than otherwise: It turns our world into a playground of possibility, choice, and empathic response rather than a jail cell of judgment, a tit-for-tat mentality, and reactivity.

Mentalomics (a.k.a. We Don't Have Endless F*cks to Give!)

The recognition that we have limited psychic energy, thus limited f*ks to give, is a well-known point made by many impressive minds, from Freud to Mark Manson to the Stoics to menopausal women everywhere.

Freud posed this idea over a hundred years ago in his economic theory of libidinal energy. To sum it up, Freud spoke about the energy we need to successfully navigate certain developmental phases and events and how problems emerge when this energy becomes cathected (stuck) and not free to continue the developmental process. This is akin to having a certain number of troops as you enter a war. Should you experience a profound loss in a particular battle, you will have fewer troops available to win the larger conflict.

I started calling this phenomenon "mentalomics" after spending a sick day watching countless episodes of *The Deadliest Catch* (more about that later in the book). It refers to the basic economy of our minds. As humans, we do not have unlimited resources, and a concept that explores the meaning of supply, demand, investment, returns, and dividends can be very helpful. I have often used this term with clients as I have them consider what battles in life in which they may have expended a great deal of energy, lost a large number of their metaphorical troops but then plowed ahead only to find themselves burned out, depleted and less than successful in pursuing their goals. I have also used this economic theory on a smaller scale to help clients consider that everything—every action, reaction, emotion, and thought process—has a cost. For example, the road rage we allow ourselves to experience on the way to an important business dinner or a complicated family dinner may leave us limping, compromised, and unable to show up well. Or if we know we have a big interview coming up, we may want to think about how much time we spend on events, external and internal, that are beyond our control in the days leading up to it. We all can name external events that are beyond our control. But what internal events are beyond our control? We can't control it if our anxious minds throw us a strange thought, a weird vibe, or our body tosses us a strange sensation (i.e., heart palpitations, dizziness, feeling faint, feeling disconnected, etc.). In fact, we can expect that in the moments leading up to either a stressful event or one in which the stakes are high, our bodies and minds might try to bluff us with discomfort so that we may back away, and/or give up and stay in a safe, predictable zone. We then must decide if we want to expend energy turning inward, giving attention to this bluff, and inadvertently feeding anxiety rather than our goals and dreams.

I love this quote from Mark Manson's book *The Subtle Art of Not Giving a F*ck:* "The key to a good life is not about giving a f*ck more; it's about giving a f*ck less, giving a f*ck about what is true, immediate and important." How do we discern what is true, immediate, and important? Well, that taps back into using wisdom to guide us. For wisdom to guide us, we must be willing to slow down and let our *wise minds* make deliberate choices about where we place our attention. So, one can see that wisdom and being discerning about where we place our limited "give a f*cks" are highly intertwined. Do we become wise by being discerning, or do we become discerning because we are wise? Yes... to both. How do we do this? We practice. And it is this practice that is a cornerstone of Stoic philosophy. We practice slowing down, we practice remembering that we have to be discerning and knowing that we can't give anything and everything our attention, our concern, and our energy. Then we choose. Sometimes we get it wrong. We use all the data—our mistakes, successes, and past experiences—to learn and refine our decisions and discernment next time.

Why did I mention menopausal women? Well, as a woman going through this crazy process, I felt totally unprepared for the level of mental and physical *f*ckery* that has accompanied it. So, as I began to do what I do—research—I found hundreds and hundreds of anecdotal comments from women who all seemed to agree that the best thing to come out of menopause was that their give-a-shit meter no longer worked. Remember Kathy Bate's character in *Fried Green Tomatoes* as she morphed from a binge-eating, people-pleasing, masochistic sobbing mess into the kick-ass, take no shit, Towanda? When I first saw the movie, I was too young to truly relate to her character and her menopausal arc. But I get it now. Boy, do I get it.

Whatever gets you there—reading the Stoics, Manson, Freud, or plummeting estrogen levels—it can be truly empowering to recognize and live by the truth that we don't have endless f*cks to give and to live our lives knowing that it is up to us (and us alone) to choose where we place that precious energy.

"The Way We Do Anything Is the Way We Do Everything."

- Marsha Beck

I can't remember when I first heard this nugget of wisdom, but I recall getting goosebumps. Goosebumps are what often happens to me when I stagger upon a profound yet unacknowledged personal truth as it speaks directly to my soul. So often in my life, I have found that as I get into a flow state in one aspect of my life—let's say exercise and self-care—suddenly, I am more efficient, more creative, and more productive across all spheres. However, when I begin to slip in an area, for example, my discipline to journal every day, I find I am less effective as a therapist, my home becomes messier, and I feel less content in my relationships.

I have also seen this play out in the lives of many of my clients. I had a client come in and describe feeling unfulfilled at work, stating he was just skating by with little effort and dedication. He couldn't understand why his marriage was failing; his relationship with his kids was less than stellar, and he found himself more prone to binge-watching television and eating more garbage. The very same part of him that would rather coast than cultivate a new skill set or set the bar higher at his current job, was the very same part that crept into what he was willing to put into his marriage, his daily practice of self-care, and his role as a parent.

That said, we can also use this statement to motivate us. If the way we do anything is actually the way we do everything, then, at any time, we can pick an area of our lives we wish to improve and begin to make a shift. Let's take the client I mentioned above and let's call him Greg. Greg was distraught as he did not feel fulfilled, motivated, or effective in any part of his life. We began to focus on one aspect at a time, and he decided he wanted to start by looking at his marriage. As he gained some skills and began to be curious about how his wife felt and what she needed, he began to build a disciplined practice towards being a more attentive husband. He began to communicate more effectively, truly listened to her when she shared about her day with the kids and carved out time for a weekly date night that she had been proposing for years. As the months passed and his marriage improved, he realized how things had also improved with the children. He was slowing down and becoming more curious about them. In turn, they were excited to see him and to share their latest news and discoveries when he walked in the door at the end of the day. He realized he enjoyed coming home and looked forward to his weekends—something that had not been the case in years. Over time, his whole demeanor changed. He lost weight without trying, his high blood pressure came down, and he felt motivated to talk to his boss about taking on some new challenges at work. When his ideas were shot down, he decided he needed a new job and found one that was not only a better fit but paid more and gave him more vacation time. In six months, he had moved from being apathetic and feeling like a failure to looking forward to life and feeling invaluable at home and work.

Often, when we find ourselves in a hole like Greg's, we either feel stuck and trapped, or we think we need to cut bait and start over. We often feel that making one minor change and choosing one thing to DO differently is like tossing a glass of water on an inferno. But you can see from this example, and I have seen it in numerous other clients I have worked with, as well as in my own life, that how we do anything is often truly how we do everything. So, choose one thing out of your *anythings* and begin tackling it with a new mindset and discipline. Then watch as it becomes almost intuitive to implement similar strategies and mindset for the rest of your life.

Because We Can

Why am I…

…always the one having to take the high road?

…always the one that does the right thing?

…always the one that should let that go?

…always the one that forgives?

…always the one that thinks to do something nice?

…always doing my part, and no one else does their part?

…always trying so hard to be a good spouse/parent/partner/colleague/friend when they don't seem to be working very hard?

Because you can.

I mentioned this phrase a few chapters back and want to expand on it a bit. When we remove the scoreboard from our game of life, when we step out of a tit-for-tat mentality—life becomes so much simpler. We are responsive rather than reactive, and our decisions are streamlined to reflect ourselves and our values rather than the myriad of circumstances that pop up around us all day, every day.

We do the right thing because of who WE are, not because of how deserving someone else is. We forgive because we value *forgiveness* and being a forgiving person. We show up well and on time and never empty-handed because we value *service to others* and being that sort of person. We take the high road because we value *doing the right thing* and not showing up small for anyone... ever. We let go because we realize and know how high the stakes are and the extent of the cost if we operate as injustice collectors in this world. We do our part because we are someone that does our part. We show up well regardless of circumstances because we value not being tossed around as a walking reaction to everyone and everything around us.

Unfortunately, this is often not how we are taught. We are taught fairness and that it's reasonable and justifiable to show up poorly towards someone who treats us poorly. Okay, so it's reasonable and justifiable. Who cares? Does reactive behavior pull us out of our value system? If so, then we lose. Not only has another person wronged us, but now we have wronged ourselves. A double whammy. Who gains from that exchange... nobody!

Imagine if we didn't have to wait around to see how others were going to behave to determine our course of action. But that's exactly what we do. We go in with good intentions, but if someone tosses a turd in our punchbowl, suddenly our good mood sours, our sense of gratitude gets replaced with revenge fantasies, and our course has been altered. Also, many of us have grown up with the belief that we should only invest in things that yield a higher return than our original investment. While that is a wise approach when it comes to money management, in the world of relationships and our responsiveness to the vicissitudes of life, it is not only short-sided but can turn us into mindless, selfish, and unhappy people. I can give you a smile, a moment of patience, a soft place to land not because it will ensure that you will give me something of equal or greater value in return, but because I realize I can make that offering and I choose to do so. Just 'cuz.

This doesn't mean we have to choose to continue to put ourselves in situations where we don't like the way people handle things, themselves, or us. We get to choose who is deserving of our time. However, way too many of us are living our lives with a sense of peace, happiness, or contentment that is only as stable as the whimsical mood of the person in front of us at the checkout line at the grocery store. If they smile and are cordial, our good mood stays intact. If they give us a strange look or are rude, we are now stomping to our cars angry and altered.

Why should I be nice to that grocery store checker when she was an asshole to me?

Because you can.

Why should I assume that someone is having a bad day and it's not personal when it certainly feels personal?

Because you can.

We are the agents of our own lives. We need to slow down and get in touch with our values. Slow down and determine our beliefs about people and life. For example: Do you believe that people are doing the best they can? Do you believe that most things aren't personal? Do you believe that life is hard and the person who just gave you a bad look or acted unkind may be being squeezed by life just a bit harder? Or do you believe that you should only offer kindness to kindness, patience for those who are patient, and generosity to those that you deem deserving? It's ultimately our choice, and there is no right or wrong answer, but I can tell you that the former certainly makes it all go so much smoother. Instead of tying our kites to someone else's string, we can go out there and fly our own kites. We can choose to show up well and be selfless, forgiving, and kind, not because we have deemed someone worthy or to get something in return—we do so *because we can.*

We Get Good at What We Practice. Period.

We Get Good at What We Practice—I would imagine 90% of anyone who has ever worked with me has heard me tout this piece of wisdom. And I would wager that 100% of them have rolled their eyes as I have said it. It's a simple truth. Simple, but certainly not easy. What we do and how we think informs our perspective... about everything! If you practice scanning for injustices, not only will you find them, but you will become masterful at sniffing them out. Then as you practice being an injustice collector, you will get good at feeling like the world and the people in it are out there taking more than their share and that things are simply unfair. On the other hand, if you practice gratitude, you will also become masterful at finding the pearl in the oyster. As you begin to scan for the spaces in your life to practice grace and gratitude, you will become good at seeing the good in yourself, in others, and in the inherent light in the world.

Are you a worry wart beginning to feel that anxiety is taking over your life? If so, surrender; practice disengaging from every thought and image that plays out on the screen in your mind. With practice, you will get good at letting things go, the worry will lessen, and the anxiety will reduce. On the other hand, if you practice taking every thought that comes across the screen seriously and treat it as an emergency and crisis, you will get good at overthinking. You will find yourself fueling the negative fire and will get good at feeling dread, doom, gloom, and distress.

Anything we have done repeatedly over a long enough period creates a neural pathway. Over time, that well-worn groove seems to take on a life of its own, and suddenly, we feel that our lives, our thoughts, and our unhealthy habits are driving the bus. To make a change, we must know what behavior, habit, or thought pattern we want to shift and then set up a practice to do something different. We may have to do that new thing a thousand times before a new neural pathway is established, but it will develop.

For example, if every morning I wake up with a bad case of what I call *the dreeps*—a cross between depression, the creeps, dread, and doom—and every morning I say to myself, *Damn, they're still here—I hate this, I want to feel normal. What if I never feel normal? What if this never goes away? What if I always feel like this? What does this feeling mean? Am I depressed? Am I broken? What if this gets worse? What if there is something really wrong with me? What if I can't handle this? I* am engaging the distressing thoughts and feelings and practicing non-acceptance and resistance. I can guarantee that this will only grow the wildly discomforting dreep state that I encounter each morning. What we feed, grows!

Instead, if I wake up and begin to practice a new mindset of, *Yep, there they are again. I know this drill. I know this is caused by tired nerves. Leave it alone… no questions to answer… nothing to see here… let's get on with the day.* I can pretty much guarantee that with this new practice over a long enough period of time, I will not be adding fear to fear. I will not be adding stress to stress, and the feelings and sensations generated by these thoughts will eventually settle.

Again, we get good at what we practice. We can be the most miserable, negative, self-absorbed, anxiety-driven person out there. Or we can practice not taking ourselves or the world so seriously and practice surrendering, letting go, and leaving things alone. It is completely within our control. It's up to us.

Changing our neural pathways requires shifts in mindset and repetition. When I was learning to play basketball, if my coach had walked in on the first day and taught us to dribble, shoot, pass, and condition and then walked out—expecting us to retain and master these new skills overnight—well, I would never have been successful at the sport. I had to decide that I wanted to learn something new and then I had to be open to the coach's instruction. Then I had to commit to practicing this new set of skills over and over and over again and then I had to practice some more. Professional musicians and athletes don't reach their dream job in the symphony or play in the NBA and then stop practicing. Why? If, after they had taken the job, they had laid down the cello or the basketball and decided to spend the next year playing video games, the neural pathway that enabled their excellence would begin to erode. In time, a new neural pathway would develop—sleeping late, making excuses, and playing video games—and they wouldn't keep their position as first chair cellist or starting point guard very long.

If we practice being a stand-up person, we are going to find opportunities to do the right thing. If we practice being an ass clown, we will also find ample opportunity to let those qualities shine through.

We need to identify our goals. We then need to look at what our current mindset and practices are that might be getting in the way of reaching those goals. We can then make a conscious decision to create a new pathway and sign a contract with ourselves to be in it for the long haul. The formula for creating change in our lives is effort over time. We tend to go wrong with one of those two variables—either we are not willing to practice (effort), or we are not willing to practice long enough (time).

The formula is simple but not easy. Making shifts is not complicated, but you have to override potential software (neural pathways) that you have been using for a very long time. Every day, we wake up and take an inventory of what we are practicing, day in and day out. Are we being a victim? An injustice collector? Judgmental? Negative? Lazy? Or are we being grateful, open to possibility, open to new ideas, and scanning for what is right and sound and good in the world? It's our choice. If we water the weeds, we can't sit and wonder why our garden is such a mess. We get good at what we practice. Period. What are you practicing?

Your Loved One Is Not Your Appendage

It is easy for many of us in our close relationships, especially in our long-term romantic relationships, to become complacent and take things for granted. At the far dysfunctional end of that scale, we stop seeing our partners or loved ones as anything more than our right hand, our eyes, our ears, and our brain. We lose sight of where we end and they begin. We want them to think the way we want them to think, act the way we want them to act, and feel the way we want them to feel. We expect them to assume our thoughts and feelings, know our next move before we make it, and show up for us without even letting them know what we need.

One time, I was working with a couple, and the husband felt that his wife was controlling as she would become upset with him when his business meetings would get extended at the last minute. "Doesn't she know I am working so hard to support our family? It's my job that allows her to travel and buy nice things."

His wife was equally upset and expressed this sentiment: "And my job is to run our home and our kids and family and when he calls me at the last minute to tell me he will be gone another night or two I have to re-arrange everything. He doesn't seem to care at all how hard it is to juggle all that I have on my plate."

In talking further with them, it was clear they were both frustrated, and both felt overlooked, undervalued, and blamed. They both ultimately wanted the same thing—for their efforts to be acknowledged, to be seen, and to feel appreciated. They were able to admit that, over the years, they had simply stopped seeing each other as separate human beings who were doing the best that they could. They had stopped checking in to see how each other was really doing. He admitted that he felt his wife *should just know* that he was as upset as she was at the last-minute business shuffling. She admitted that she felt her husband *should know how hard it is to keep the home running, especially when new variables regarding schedules entered the scene.*

Thinking our partners and loved ones *should just know* is a problem. We need to take responsibility to share openly about what we want and need in our relationships. I am not saying it wouldn't be amazing once in a while for our partners to just nail it; just read our minds, see inside our hearts, and know exactly what we need. That's a gift when that happens. But when life is going 190 mph, it is often hard to slow down and be able to do this. We have to be willing to ask for what we need. We have to be willing to recognize when we have stopped seeing our partners or loved ones as individuals with wants, needs, moods, fears, limits, and vulnerabilities.

Most couples I work with will describe how it "used to be." If we can put down the blaming, the projection, and the expectations for just a moment, we can usually find the tender spot of grief. What each is missing from the other, what has been lost along the way, and begin to work on a way back to each other.

Another woman I worked with once told me, "If I tell him what I want for my birthday and then he gets it for me, how will I know it wasn't because I asked for it? It wouldn't have been his idea; it wouldn't have come from him." This is a trap. Whether we are talking about material gift giving or how someone shows up, choosing to withhold what you want and need to see if they would have gotten it right on their own—that's a game. A game that typically ends with a great deal of frustration and resentment.

I did not agree with the sentiment in the movie *Jerry McGuire*, "You complete me." Nope. The relationships that I've seen work are the ones where both people are complete in and of themselves. They work interdependently and rely on each other but do not need their partner to complete them on an emotional level. They might (and hopefully do) enjoy their life even more with this person by their side. They want their relationship to succeed, and they do so by dropping blame and projection. The successful couples I know are aware of where they end and the other begins. They aren't into testing their partner to see if they will get it right. They help their partners get it right. They speak up. They are direct and kind in their wants and needs. They are aware of their partner's vulnerabilities as well as the reality that it isn't always going to run smoothly. Their partner is not the other half of their brain, their right arm, or their mind reader. They do not treat their partner as an appendage but as the person that they have consciously decided to walk through life with, and they can see them as separate, self-sustaining beings who have decided to stay and walk through life with them as well. When our partners become our right arm, we can no longer see them. We can only see ourselves, our wants, our needs, our desires, our frustrations, and our anger.

Step back, slow down, and take a bird's-eye view. And remember, no one should know you better than you know yourself. And one thing we know about ourselves is that we are always changing and evolving. This includes our wants, desires, needs, fears, and hopes. So, stop being hurt when your partner gets it wrong. Before you start heading down the resentment slide, slow down and ask yourself if you are testing your loved one. If so, stop it; he or she is not your pupil. Work to be aware of yourself and mindfully remind yourself that someone has chosen you specifically out of this great big world to join them in their journey through life. If you keep this point in the forefront of your mind, you will be surprised how fresh and healthy the relationship can remain over a lifetime.

Between Stimulus and Response There Is a Space...

One of the most powerful quotes out there is credited to Viktor Frankl, Austrian psychologist, author, and Holocaust survivor. The full quote is: "Between stimulus and response there is a space. In that space is our power to choose our response. In our response lies our growth and our freedom."

Sometimes that space between the stimulus and response is difficult to find. For example, if someone is berating, mistreating, or trying to intimidate us it may appear that there is no space to choose between that offense and our tears/anger/fear. But that is the key moment to slow down. The act of finding that space is what needs to be practiced. If we practice being a walking reaction to what happens around us and to us, we will get good at it. If we practice slowing down and looking for that space, trusting that it is there and knowing then that it is fully up to us how we choose to show up and respond—we will eventually get good at this as well.

Over the years, many clients would come to their appointments feeling overwhelmed and beaten down by life. They would often feel hopeless, helpless, and wildly unhappy with their life's circumstances and a sense of having lost themselves in negativity and fear. The work for most is quite simple but not easy. Quite simple in that all we had to do to unlock their self-agency was to locate that space. The space between their adverse life events (troubled marriage, bad job, illness, injury, abuse) and their response (fear, terror, resentment, frustration, panic). It is often in these situations that folks are encouraged to look deep and long into their pasts to uncover some sort of pattern or early life event that has led to their current unhappiness. While that may prove to be interesting and helpful, it can also result in diving down another rabbit hole and remaining stuck and miserable.

What if instead, in the here and now, we are taught to simply slow down to the speed of wisdom, realize, and consciously decide that there is always a choice? We can choose to keep looking for someone to blame (and we will usually always find someone), and we may not be wrong. But at what cost? Blame is expensive. It robs us of our time and our energy. There may actually be someone or some event responsible for the conditions of our hardship. Let me repeat that: There may actually be someone or some event responsible for the conditions of our hardship. That is vastly different from there being someone or some event that is responsible for how we RESPOND to our challenging life circumstances or hardships.

Again, squeeze me, and "Jen Juice" comes out. It doesn't matter if what squeezed us was a mean boss, a bad traffic jam, crappy childhood, or a scary medical diagnosis. We are still responsible. And because we are still responsible, we are free. And in being free, we can then freely choose to give up, blame, or remain frustrated, or we can choose to find meaning, show up well, and infuse a bad set of circumstances with wisdom and grace. Remarkably simple. Not easy. Not easy because we live in a world where projection and scapegoating are replacing personal responsibility thus leading to a disavowal of our own power. We seek to punish, blame, and attribute the unfairness of our lives to someone else, but it is sand out of our own hourglass that is being lost by remaining locked in this mindset. So, it is true that to choose to stay on our own side of the street and make it our mission to be responsible for locating that space between the various stimuli/situations in our life and our response to them is not an easy or popular task. But it is a powerful skill that will set one apart from the pack.

What You Tolerate, You Validate

Often in my practice, I will have clients who will come to me beaten down and battle-weary due to problematic and exhausting dynamics in their marriage, or with their children, in their workplace, or with their extended family. These clients not only need support and a place to vent, but they also need to be reminded of their agency in the situation. If we tolerate our partner snapping at us or putting us down, we are validating that they have a right to do so and that we aren't worth more than the dismissive manner in which they are treating us. Suppose we allow our children to rule the roost and tolerate their bad manners. In that case, we are validating their behavior and teaching them that disrespecting other people's feelings and space is okay. If we stick around as our spouse doesn't take their alcoholism seriously—tolerating frightening periodic benders that leave us frazzled and frustrated—we are validating that we support their lack of commitment and showing them that there are no relational consequences for their actions.

I was working with a lovely woman whose husband often came home late, was elusive about where he had been, reeking of alcohol, and was verbally abusive to her. She came to see me and stated, "I'm at the end of my rope." She went on to say, "If he loved me, he would change."

While I could see the exhaustion plastered over her entire being, I had to ask, "So tell me about this rope." She seemed perplexed, so I explained, "You said you are at the end of it, so what exactly is the rope? I'm assuming there is something you have been doing, saying, wishing, asking, and are tired of doing so now?" She thought for a moment and explained how, for years, she had been asking him to check in with her if he was going to be later than expected. Sometimes he would, sometimes he wouldn't. For years she had been trying to get him to stop being so elusive and come clean about where he had been. Sometimes he would, sometimes he wouldn't. For years she had threatened to leave if he continued to come home drunk and pick a fight or verbally berate her. On a few occasions, she left for an hour or two. Once, she left for a day.

I then asked her about her second comment: *If he loved me, he would change.* She said, "Yes if he loved me, he would stop this. He knows how upsetting it is to me."

I then said, "And this has been going on for years?" She nodded, fighting back tears. While I had and felt great empathy for this woman, she needed to ask herself some tough questions. So, I asked, "If you loved you, what would you change about this situation?"

She immediately became defensive and said, "This isn't about me, I love myself just fine—this is about him."

I told her I respectfully disagreed. While it involved him and his refusal to respect her requests and limits, it was very much about her and the agreement she was making with herself to tolerate his behavior and treatment. We are what we allow. We show people how we expect to be treated. While we would all love to never be put in a position to forcefully hold a line or limit, the fact is if we want to be treated well, we have to command that respect. Commanding that respect starts and ends with having that respect for ourselves. There will be people in our lives who can join us and continue the journey with us, and there will be those who have no intention of respecting our limits and needs. We are not responsible for somebody else's bad behavior. We are, however, completely responsible for how we let that behavior impact our own quality of life.

Fast forward nine months, and things have been vastly different for this client. Two weeks after our second meeting, her husband came home late, drunk, and began to pick a fight and verbally berate her. She packed up the kids and spent the weekend with a friend. She stood her ground and said that she would only consider remaining in the marriage if he would agree to a temporary separation, intense couples counseling, and if he would agree to work actively on his drinking. While he initially resisted, she held her ground, validating herself and her limits, and because of this gained valuable information about her marriage and herself. To this day, they are married; she has reclaimed her voice and self-respect, he altered his behavior, and they continue to actively work on their marriage and family.

Granted, I understand this is not always how these things turn out. Sometimes we have to let people go. Sometimes, people won't do the hard work. And sometimes, we ourselves need a reality check to determine if our *limits* are actually reasonable given the situation. Again, as the title suggests—just because they push your buttons doesn't mean they are responsible for them. However, if we have spent some time reflecting and checking our blind spots with a trusted, unbiased source and we still determine that our limits are not unreasonable and are necessary for our quality of life—then we have to ask ourselves the tough questions; *What am I validating by tolerating this behavior?* ... and... *What role do I have in perpetuating this challenging situation?*

In my own life, I have been guilty of putting up with things from people that undermined my own basic self-respect. On occasion, I would find myself in the victim role pointing fingers and saying, "But look at what they are doing?"

One day I reached out to a friend, and she said the hard but important words, "No, look at what you are allowing." I didn't want to hear it, but she was right. I was so busy feeling sorry for myself and focused on the unfairness of the situation that I lost sight of my own contribution to the problem. We all need friends, guides, coaches, and therapists that are a safe place to land. But sometimes we also need someone to care enough about us to hold up a mirror and ask us the tough questions. So, if there is something you have allowed to continue despite it going against your values or affecting your quality of life, what are you validating by doing so, and how is that working out for you? Remember, this is our time slot here on Earth. The only one promised as far as we know. We get to say where we end, and another person begins. Because if we don't say it, believe me—someone else will.

"Everything Will Be Okay, When I Am Okay With Everything."

- Michael Singer

I will never forget when I read this quote in Michael Singer's book *The Untethered Soul*. I was sitting on the porch of my parent's lake house in Northeastern PA. It was a beautiful sunny day in the summer of 2015. I was happy enough in my life. I had a great family, great friends, and a great career. There were plenty of hardships in that 45th year of life, but I was mostly content. I was for sure happy to be on vacation and doing what I loved most (reading) at one of my most favorite places (The Pocono Mountains.) Then I read this quote. I got instant goosebumps. As mentioned earlier, goosebumps are what I believe to be *truth* telling my soul, *hey this is important.*

I read this quote many times and I remember feeling instantly nauseous and saying, aloud and to no one, "I wish I hadn't read that line." For weeks I couldn't shake it. *How does someone get okay with everything? How does someone get okay with a family member dying early from a terrible disease? How does someone get okay with war and tragedy?* My mind raced and my head ached. I also distinctly remember sensing that I had stumbled upon that line for a reason. That my goosebumps weren't an accident and that I would be faced with the choice of getting okay with everything (or not) at some point. I didn't know what was in store for me. I won't go into the details of what exactly happened—that's chronicled in my book *The Waiting Room.* But the quick Readers Digest version is that I took a medication as prescribed and had a terrible adverse reaction that was deemed a rare, neurotoxic injury that led to a slew of neurological issues that waxed and waned for years. During that experience, there were times I no longer wanted to live. I hurt and struggled in a manner that felt beyond humane and the only words I could think of to explain the depths of the despair I felt was the annihilation of self. I saw Hell. I wish I were being hyperbolic in saying that. But it is the only way I can describe that period of my life.

As I worked to reclaim my life, my health, and my sanity, Michael Singer's words returned to my conscious awareness. I began to realize that the hellish journey had trimmed the fat off my lived experience. It had ripped off my mask and left me raw and vulnerable. When you hit the edge of your own sanity and your own existence and don't swing the other leg over and jump off, it's amazing what you find in yourself and realize about the world as you stick around. I don't want to lose a loved one, don't want to ever be that sick again, and don't want people I care about to ever feel hurt, humiliation, pain, or angst. But I know that I will be okay. And because I can be okay with whatever happens during this earthly life, I am free. I am free to truly be okay.

This doesn't mean that we must like feeling anxious or depressed. It doesn't mean we are immune to the injustices and circumstances of the world. It simply means that we radically accept that we are strong enough to allow bad shit to occur. We can certainly do our part to not create injustice and to fight for what we believe in. But at the end of the day, we realize that we are not in control of much and we surrender. We don't quit. We surrender. We stop trying to push that boulder up the hill. We stop taking on the responsibility for the feelings and happiness of everyone around us. We allow people to learn their lessons and for natural consequences to occur. Don't get me wrong, I can still resist and turn myself into a pretzel about many things. But now Michael's words come to me more quickly. I am able to notice when I am being resistant or controlling much faster and I am better at dropping the rope sooner rather than later.

What are you resisting? What are you working so hard to control? Can you imagine becoming okay with everything? If you find yourself quickly saying NO—hold tight for a minute. Don't be so quick to dismiss this idea. I don't want you to have to endure a dark night of the soul to experience the power in this statement. Slow down and think about what you need to get okay with. Do your own surrender experiment. I promise it won't be a waste of your time.

Is It a Relationship or a Hostage Situation?

Sound familiar?

...I can't leave them because what if they hurt themselves?

...I can't stop paying for everything because they won't take care of themselves.

...I can't hold that limit I set because I fear they won't fight for me or the relationship.

...I am afraid to say no because I know there will be hell to pay.

...I am afraid to leave because I need to be here to keep them from drinking.

...I am afraid to leave because they will spread lies about me to our family and friends.

...I am afraid to speak my mind because I know they will turn it around on me.

...I can't seem to get anything right; I'm always having to walk on eggshells.

...I'm always getting blamed no matter how hard I try.

...I don't like the person I become when I'm around them.

...I don't recognize myself any longer.

These are just a few of the many things I have heard from clients who feel trapped in their relationship. For some, it's a romantic relationship; for others, it's with their adult child, a parent, sibling, other family member, or boss.

For years I worked with a gentleman whose thirty-two-year-old daughter had been diagnosed with a personality disorder. He financed her life fully and often ended gratifying relationships with women because of his daughter's suicidal threats, stating she felt rejected, abandoned, and replaced when he began to date. He hated answering calls from her; one day things would go smoothly, and she would be kind and the next day she would spend hours berating him for never being there for her, not loving her, and being a terrible parent and human being. Her mother had left them when she was thirteen years old and in our first session, he spoke about the extreme guilt he felt due to her mother's abandonment and his desperate attempts to make it up to her.

During our first few sessions, I noticed he kept looking at his phone which was vibrating incessantly. On one occasion he even stepped out to take a call. When I asked him about it, he said that his daughter knew he was starting therapy and was feeling somewhat threatened. I asked him if she knew what time our appointment was scheduled for, and he nodded meekly. When I asked him why he had felt compelled to take the call he said, "She might have killed herself if I didn't answer." He hadn't even taken a moment to consider his response. Those were the stakes he had been living with for years. Morning, day, middle of the night, on a business trip, home ill, out golfing, it didn't matter; he had learned the hard way that he better always be available to her. He explained that years earlier, while away on a business trip, he was giving a talk to a group of investors and had missed her call. She left a text message saying "Goodbye" and then turned her phone off. Desperate to reach her, he had sent the police to her apartment for a welfare check, but she had disappeared. He left the conference early and flew home desperate and distraught. It was only a few days later, when charges from a fancy hotel down the street from her apartment showed up on his credit card, that he realized his daughter was, in fact, safe. He wept as he spoke about his exhaustion and how trapped he felt. He asked if I had ever heard of such a complicated relationship.

I remember looking at him and saying, "This is no relationship; you are a hostage." I shared with him that his guilt-driven responses to his daughter for a crime he didn't commit—his wife/her mother's decision to walk away—were interrupting a particularly important process for his daughter:

her right to grieve and decide how she was going to respond to her unfortunate life experience. Her choice was to figure out what to do with the fact that her mother had left her, as well as what to do with the reality that her father had not. I went on to explain that while he was here to guide his daughter, he could not alter reality, and he was not responsible for anyone else's response to their life circumstances—including his own child's.

This example is extreme, but I have seen so many variations of this with so many people I have worked with over the years: parents who have kids addicted to drugs or alcohol; partners who find themselves in a narcissistically abusive relationship; and adult kids who can't individuate and take up their lives because they fear their parents will cease to exist without them.

Sometimes we must be willing to face our biggest fear in order to move out of the position of being held hostage. We cannot keep another human being alive. We are not solely responsible for making someone happy, keeping them healthy, sober, or vertical and breathing. I have had to work with parents who have had to sit with their fear of knowing that their child may, in fact, commit suicide. I cannot imagine a worse pain for a parent. However, a close second is being held hostage by someone who plays the suicide card to keep you jumping through hoops.

I have had to work with many people as they do the work to free themselves and to let their loved ones go. They don't have to stop loving them, but they have to step out of the cage that has been created and really embrace the harsh reality that they, themselves, may be participating in having become or remaining a hostage.

Our lives are not intended to be never-ending, eggshell-walking, soul-sucking groundhog days of fear. And it's up to us to account for the energy we are expending in our relationships with other people and the toll it takes on us. Don't expect the person holding you hostage to see it for what it is. Don't expect them to not put up a fight when you command respect through changes in your behavior. The only people who really fight and resist us when we establish limits and boundaries are the ones who are not served by them being in place. *No* is a complete sentence. And you can decide that something is not serving you and make necessary changes without getting permission. In fact, what often keeps so many stuck is trying to have a conversation for the thousandth time explaining why they might be establishing said boundary or limit. Say it once. Don't expect a parade; expect a fight. Stop explaining and do what needs to be done. No one is coming to save you. It's harsh but true. If you are a hostage, realize that you and you alone hold the key to that cage. And it will be you and you alone that will choose to use the key, step outside, and choose to be courageous in taking up your life and allowing your loved one to take up theirs in whatever form or fashion they see fit.

The Stockdale Paradox

Ever find yourself in a situation or set of circumstances where things feel bleak, hopeless, and painful beyond what you feel you can endure? Enter James Stockdale. James Stockdale was an admiral in the US Navy and was awarded the Medal of Honor in the Vietnam War, during which he spent SEVEN years as a prisoner of war. Seven years!

I am not sure where I first heard about the Stockdale Paradox—it may have been from one of Ryan Holiday's books or blogs—but I remember getting goosebumps after I read about this courageous man and his paradoxical philosophy that he credits for his survival during those seven years.

In essence, the paradox was one of hope and radical acceptance. Many of the other POWs would think *I just have to hang on, and I'll be out of here by Christmas,* or *I know I'll be out of here by my next birthday, just have to hang on.* Then, unfortunately, Christmas would come and go, or their birthday would pass by unnoticed with no change and these men would become disheartened and even more battle-weary. Stockdale took a slightly different approach. He maintained a strong belief that he would be free—one day. But would say to himself something like this: *While I know I will one day be free, today is not that day. So today I have to do whatever it takes to survive.*

When I was going through an incredibly challenging health condition, these words gave me great direction and comfort. In my most trying moments, I would say to myself, *I know one day I will be healed. But today is clearly not that day. Tomorrow is most likely not that day either. For now, I have to do what it takes to remain vertical and breathing and stay focused on the moment.*

What trials and tribulations, dark nights of the soul, and trying circumstances have you found yourself in? Can you imagine working to employ these words? For me, they offered a great deal of stability, practical realism, and direction. Even if the only direction on any given day was to stay vertical and breathing.

Like the Stockdale Paradox, another perspective shifter I suggest to clients who are facing severe distress due to illness or circumstance is what I call a "Deal with the Devil." In my most bleak moments, I would imagine some powerful malevolent force coming to me and promising me full recovery and instant healing. I wouldn't have to spend one more moment scared, in pain, or distress. The only catch was that as soon as I shed my cloak of despair and pain, it would be immediately transferred to one of my parents or other family members. I would spend the rest of my life free and healthy but would have to stand by and watch someone I dearly loved as they absorbed and took on my suffering. Every single time I would think about this, even in my most desperate times, I would say, *No deal!* Then I would return to the wisdom of James Stockdale and carry on.

Sometimes when things are dark, bleak, or simply wildly overwhelming, we can begin to lose hope. We can feel so desperate, we say we would do ANYTHING to rid ourselves of the distress. As morose and morbid as it may sound, using this approach shifted my perspective nearly immediately. I could almost hear myself being asked, "Are you sure? Are you sure you can handle this, Jen? Because you can tap out right now." But, for me, and I believe for so many of us, while they say the worst kind of pain is your own pain, every fiber in my being would rather take the hit than watch someone that I love have to carry that burden for even a day.

So, whether you draw from Admiral Stockdale's amazing courage, find some leverage in imagining your own "Deal with the Devil," or devise a tactic of your own, it is imperative to always be searching for that pivot point where we can shift our perspective and reclaim some agency and grounding in the dark moments of our lives.

"Get Busy Living or Get Busy Dying."

- Andy Dufresne
(The Shawshank Redemption)

My. Favorite. Movie. I remember getting another round of my infamous goosebumps when Andy said these words to Red leaning up against the prison wall. Another *truth* bumping up against my soul. I heard these words at a critical time in my life. A time when I was feeling somewhat lost and confused.

This is it guys. This is our time slot. A slot we didn't earn. The slot we have been granted. One that is not guaranteed to be long and luxurious. Its only guarantee is that it is ours. We can do all sorts of things with this time slot, and I realized when I heard Andy say those words that I had spent much of my time slot over the years waiting. Waiting for life to begin. Does that make sense? Almost waiting for permission. I can get in shape, reach that goal, take on that project, feel comfortable in my skin, try that thing when... when what?

So many of my clients arrive at my door feeling depressed, anxious, overwhelmed, underwhelmed, obsessive, compulsive, bored, angry, sad, and lost. A prevailing theme I find in many of their lives is that they too are lying in wait. Waiting for life to come and find them, pick them up, dust them off, and send them on their way. Guess what? No one is coming to save us. That's the bad news and the good news. It is up to us.

Martin was a middle-aged man who came to see me to deal with the grief over the break-up of his marriage. He blamed himself for the break-up and it had been six years since the divorce by the time he landed in my office. He had been to several therapists before me. One had died, one had moved, and one had retired. Martin repeatedly played out the final years of his marriage where he described himself as checked out, addicted to porn, food, and alcohol, and *phoning it in* with his kids. I asked if he currently, six years later, felt more present in his life. *Nope.* I asked if he still watched porn, ate, and drank compulsively? *Yep.* I asked if he still phoned it in with his kids. *Kinda.*

Every week for a few months, Martin would come in and make a new plan. A new plan that included looking for a new job, starting to work out, attending a recovery meeting for sex addiction, building in more fun, engaging activities, and spending more time with his two teenage sons. By day three or four of nearly every week, the plan had fallen apart. There was always an excuse: "My sons didn't want to go bowling or golfing; I had to work late the night of the SA meeting; I had to go out to two business dinners and it's impossible to eat well and not drink when I have to entertain."

After a few months, I asked Martin not to schedule another appointment with me. I explained that he had a decision to make. I actually used Andy's phrase and said, "Martin, you need to get busy living or get busy dying. Which one do you think you are doing right now?" He knew the answer but still left my office upset and frustrated with me. I didn't hear from Martin for over four months. One day as I was locking up, I walked out and found him sitting on a bench outside of my office. He looked like the world had chewed him up and spit him out.

He said, "I'm ready to start living."

The next week we resumed our work. Martin stopped phoning it in with both his children and in his therapy. He worked hard at developing value-driven behaviors and activities. He practiced patience and restraint as I encouraged him to start small and build slow and steady. A year later Martin was in a new job, had lost forty pounds, attended a weekly SA meeting, made amends with his ex-wife, and was planning a three-week trip to Europe with his sons for his oldest son's graduation gift.

Are you phoning it in at work? In your relationship? With yourself? Are you waiting for life to come and find you? It may be time to tap into some Shawshank wisdom and ask yourself the pivotal question: Are you busy living or dying?

We're Not in Kansas Anymore

When I was growing up as a kid in the 70s and early 80s, *The Wizard of Oz* and *Willy Wonka and the Chocolate Factory* would come on TV once a year. All year long, I would look forward to and wait for the telecast. I would scan the TV guide, make sure we would be home, and plan for the big event. There was no way we could record it to watch again, much less stream it from any number of devices in our homes. I was sad when it was over because I knew I had to start the waiting and anticipation all over again. What I was wholly unaware of were the skills I was developing in the process. I'm not suggesting we return to the "good ole days." However, there is truth in the fact that there were a lot of positive mental health benefits and neural development happening as a result of not being able to get what we wanted, when we wanted it, on whatever device was most convenient.

In today's world, for many of us, the idea of even sitting through a commercial often feels like an annoyance for our impatient minds. Skills such as tolerating frustration and distress and having the capacity to delay gratification are eroding quickly. As a result, we are losing our imagination, creativity, and our capacity to cope. We are also becoming compulsive and expectant in our approach to daily life. We get frustrated when our Amazon delivery isn't there in 48 hours. Our kids can't fathom waiting days, weeks, or months for a favorite movie or show—why should they have to when we can stream it on demand from one of our five devices? Kids today don't play *make-believe* or *pretend* games any longer. Every conceivable fantasy can be played out in vivid detail on the screen in front of them or in the palm of their hands. The creative process in their minds is never birthed because it has already been developed by somebody in Silicon Valley and delivered to them with a mouse click or a swipe of their finger. They are just playing *somebody else's* imaginary games.

All this convenience comes at a cost not just for our children, but for us as well. There are videos all over social media with people asking if anyone else feels *blah, unmotivated, lost,* and *not excited about much in life.* People are complaining of feeling empty with nothing seeming to matter much. Others are talking about feeling terribly stressed and caught on a hamster wheel that is spinning out of control. FOMO (fear of missing out) is now thought of as an emotional state.

When we had to wait, anticipate, plan, and look forward to things, we were building up emotional scar tissue. When we have to actually take the time to call up the fact that is temporarily eluding us rather than rushing to Google, we are exercising our brain.

The world is going 190 mph, and we feel we can't keep up. There is an information overload that is moving at a much faster pace than our minds and bodies can absorb. Patience and thoughtful deliberation are being replaced with impatience and impulsiveness. We are constantly being lit up by so much data, that we feel compelled to react and cast judgment on whatever's in front of us and tend to quickly move on to make sure we don't let anything pass us by. Things like discourse, agreeing to disagree, gathering more information, and being curious about a different view or perspective just simply take too long. We don't have time for it. Why? Because we are losing our capacity to slow down. Curiosity takes time and effort. The technological boom that has spawned so much efficiency has diminished our opportunities to reason, reflect, and contemplate—the building blocks we use to develop our coping skills.

While we will never go back to a time when we had to wait a year to watch our favorite show or wait six weeks for something we have ordered from a TV commercial to arrive, we can begin to employ some strategies to begin to exercise and train our brain to delay gratification and tolerate frustration. Will you and your children potentially feel a sense of discomfort should you decide to *power down* on occasion? Yes. And then guess what? Then you get to practice tolerating that as well.

World-class sprinter and Olympian, Usain Bolt said, "I trained four years for nine seconds"—now that's a disciplined mind and body—no short-term gain, no immediate reward. We may not all be Olympic athletes, but we all have the ability to achieve remarkable things if we can train our minds to work for us. We can run our lives, rather than our lives running us. We can train our neurotransmitters to operate in balance again rather than in the wild surges and dips of dopamine that occur as we hammer-scroll, insta-purchase, and "like" or "cancel" data (and people) at lightning speed.

So, take some time and look at your life and how you and your family are living. Challenge yourself to slow down and truly develop some new neural pathways that can bring long-term joy rather than short-term bursts of euphoria. Technology has created screen addicts out of most of us. It is up to us to determine how to use that tech to our advantage while being aware that even the best of tools can become weapons depending on how they are used.

Toxic People

How do we know if a relationship is *toxic*? How do we know if it's time to cut our losses and leave? If we can't walk away for whatever reason, how do we set boundaries to minimize the impact of the toxicity? Let's start with a few ways to know if you are in a relationship with a toxic person:

- Toxic people hold us hostage by not being able to let us go but also not being able to stay, show up, and treat us well.

- Toxic people berate us for our reaction to their mean, manipulative, bad, or abusive behavior.

- Toxic people take delight in our missteps, mishaps, and challenging times.

- Toxic people appear to be curious, but it is simply a way to keep tabs on their measuring stick to make sure you haven't moved too far ahead or have something they want and don't have.

- Toxic people see your gain as their loss.

- Toxic people will take a positive experience or happy time and sour it for you (ruining holidays, picking a fight while you are on a trip with friends or family).

- Toxic people stonewall (go radio silent and ice you out).

- Toxic people manipulate situations to ensure they are always the victim.

- Toxic people will be initially attracted to your kindness and empathy but then use it against you and see it as a sign of weakness.

- Toxic people tend to be pathologically certain and make a lot of assumptions that they view as "fact." *Their* perception *is* reality!

- A toxic relationship can often be described as "The good is so good I can't live without it, but the bad is so bad I am not sure I will survive it."

This is certainly not an exhaustive list, but it's a good start. I don't actually love the word toxic to describe a person. I tend to think people who fall into these patterns of behavior are hurt people who don't value self-reflection. And we know the old but true adage "Hurt people hurt people."

This is certainly not an excuse for shitty behavior. In fact, in my clinical work, I have found that many of my clients stick around in the hurt (aka toxicity) because their empathy—once an asset and now a weapon—keeps them feeling guilty and stuck. Their anger, fear, and frustration often yield much too quickly, and they end up making excuses for their loved one by saying things like "They are acting this way because of their bad childhood, tough life, etc." or even berating themselves for being *needy* or asking for *too much*. Now this may seem that I am contradicting my own advice to give people the benefit of the doubt. I'm not. I stand by giving people the benefit of the doubt as well as offering up some space and grace for less than stellar behavior at times. The operative phrase here is AT TIMES. There is a big difference between someone having a bad moment or time in their life versus sticking around in a long-term bad dynamic in which your own sense of self begins to elude you.

In a toxic dynamic, as their sense of self has been whittled down, my clients will often describe feeling like they are "breaking down." They begin to lose their sense of self, their self-confidence and esteem erode, and they become a shell of the person they once were. I have watched as they begin to twist their reality and hold on tightly to the crumb that is periodically tossed their way. Savoring it and seeing it through a distorted lens depicting that crumb as a glorious three-tiered cake that is just around the corner waiting for them.

It can be particularly challenging to break away from a person who behaves or shows up in these toxic ways. Besides compromising our reality, we can feel like we can't live without them. We can become so battle-weary that we're unable to recognize the soul fatigue for what it is. We stay because we have lost our confidence or simply started to believe that this must be all we deserve.

At the very least, we need to talk to someone outside of the toxic paradigm and allow some reality testing to occur. As we begin to see things more clearly and as we recognize the emotional carnage that has become our lives, we can begin to set limits and boundaries. And if the dynamics of the relationship don't resolve favorably, we can decide to step away altogether.

The Necessity of Consequences

There are many magnificent quotes on consequences, but I like this one by David Viscott: "To fail is a natural consequence of trying, to succeed takes time and prolonged effort in the face of unfriendly odds. To think it will be any other way, no matter what you do, is to invite yourself to be hurt and to limit your enthusiasm for trying again." I love that first sentence—to fail is a natural consequence of trying. I have spent the majority of my career doing family therapy in one form or another. Over the years I began to track a trend that was getting progressively worse. As a result, I began to see more and more problems arise. What was this trend? Parents being too afraid to let their child fail.

Of course, it is heartbreaking to watch your child not be picked for the team, not make the All-Star team, not get cast in the play, not get asked to the dance, have a falling out with a friend, or not get accepted into the college of their choice.

Ironically, this consequence—the consequence of heartbreak—is what we sign on to endure when we bring another person into this world and promise to help guide them in their lives. We make a pact to walk beside this little person as they stumble, bumble, and fall throughout their lives. Our job is to not only teach them lessons via adhering to the consequences we set such as curfews, dinner table rules, and how others are to be treated, but to allow for natural consequences to occur as well. As we allow them to stumble, bumble, and fall we do so with the deep-seated trust that the resulting scar tissue and wisdom that develops will only serve to strengthen them. This does not mean that we abandon our post. We stand next to them, breathe deep, swallow our desire to control variables, and show them that we trust they can withstand disappointment and pain.

I have also seen parents set a consequence and then backpedal on it because they cannot handle the distress as they over-empathize with their child's fear and disappointment. *Yes, I know they didn't study and get their algebra grade up, but all of their friends are going to this party. I told him he would be grounded, but I didn't realize it was the biggest party of the school year. I walk every morning with some of his friends' moms and they think I could start the punishment on Monday. I would hate for him to miss out.*

The way we truly abandon our children is when we don't teach them how to develop the capacity to anticipate consequences to make informed choices regarding their behavior.

How can they develop this insight if parents don't follow through with the consequences they have set up? It is also hurtful to our children when we communicate to them that we don't feel they can handle a consequence, such as not making a team or not making an "A," by constantly intervening and interrupting the process. Years ago, I began working on a book called *On Becoming a Person of Record.* One day I will finish that project. However, a huge premise of the book was focusing on what we as parents, guardians, aunts, uncles, teachers, and adults need to be willing to do to help our children grow into self-respecting, autonomous human beings. Being able to allow and tolerate natural consequences and the willingness to enforce the consequences we have established, is essential to raising emotionally healthy children. This is how we teach kids what it means to have integrity with their words. Delivering to them the message that life is not always fair, that we need to choose our behaviors and responses wisely, and to keep trying because failing, and missing the mark, is all simply a part of the journey towards a healthy adult life.

By the way, for all of us big kids out there, we need to make sure we are doing the same in our adult relationships. I have sat with many couples over the years where one or the other continues to threaten divorce *if you ever cheat again... don't stop drinking... don't start having sex with me... don't start communicating with me...* or *don't start pulling your weight.* Week after week, they drop the threat of the "D-bomb," and

week after week, as their partner does not change their behavior, they just threaten some more. After a while, the
word *divorce* no longer holds any weight. Their partner no
longer believes them, and they begin to feel their sense of self
slipping away as they lose respect for themselves. Don't
threaten a consequence or action without the resolve to follow
through. The consequence of setting empty consequences is a
betrayal of yourself and your word. The veiled threat of a
consequence is just as unhealthy as making false promises.
Say what you mean and mean what you say. Use wisdom to
guide you in establishing your limits. Trust that natural consequences are often the most valuable tools in creating the
changes we or others need to make in our lives. Be a person
of record, and if you are a parent—raise a person of record.
It's certainly the road less traveled, but it will make all the
difference.

Rupture and Repair

One thing every human being can count on as they navigate their various relationships is that ruptures will occur. We will hurt people's feelings; we will not always attune perfectly to someone's wants or needs. We will misstep, make mistakes, show up poorly, and disappoint people at some point. What most people don't understand is that it is typically not the rupture that is the problem, it is the repair, or more specifically, the lack of repair that causes the greatest damage.

Just because ruptures are inevitable, does not mean that we don't strive to do our best in our relationships. Part of doing our best is being humble enough to own our mistakes and apologize. And guess what? We are never too old for that apology to make a dramatic difference.

I was working with a woman who was upset and angry with her father for bringing multiple women into her life after her mom passed away. He remarried four times. My client had been devastated when her father missed her wedding to attend the wedding of his third wife's adult son. His excuse had been, "We got their invitation first, hon." She was hurt that he had left her at home alone on her sixteenth birthday with his second wife while he went golfing in California. She recalled this woman not even acknowledging her birthday and her father not calling from his trip but running out to buy her a car a week later when he realized that he had let her big day slip his mind.

I asked my client, "Let's say your dad called you right now and told you that he had been thinking about you and the many years that had passed since your mom died. He said he wanted to reach out and tell you he was sorry and how hard that must have been for you. What would that be like for you?"

My client got tears in her eyes and said, "That would never happen… and it wouldn't make it all go away… but it would mean a lot to me."

A key factor to consider when there has been a rupture in our lives with someone we care about is *conflict* versus *deficit*. While I will expand on this concept in more detail in a later chapter, in a nutshell: Conflict means the person hurts us because of something about us or our dynamic with them; whereas deficit means that they lack the capacity to give us what we need. When I asked my client about her dad and the conflict versus deficit model, her first response was "Well, he certainly had a lot to give his multitude of stepchildren and all of his wives." But as she continued, she began to describe a man who often used money and gifts as emotional currency. She was able to say, "It was my mom who was the emotionally intelligent and available one. I think Dad probably means well, but there is a reason he has been married five times. There is a reason his stepchildren only call him when they need something from him." Over time, my client was able to recognize that while it didn't take the hurt away, realizing that she wanted something from her dad that he didn't seem capable of giving to anyone seemed to soften the blow. It provided context for her dad's absence in her life. Upon further reflection, she spoke about how his parents had left him with an aunt and uncle while they went to volunteer overseas when he was three. They returned when he was six, but he continued to spend most of his time with various aunts and uncles and was passed around on the holidays while his parents spent their time building wells in less developed countries and helping less fortunate children.

We cannot offer something we don't have. Her father didn't have a model of an interested, available parent. He had married the right woman (her mother) and before she died, she was often there to help guide him into being the man and the father she believed he could be. After she passed, he was lost at sea once again.

Again, while these reflections and revelations didn't change her own past experiences, she was able to recognize that the ruptures had, in large part, occurred as a result of a huge emotional and relational deficit in her father. Not because of some lack of worth within herself.

Getting back to the idea of repair, not only this client but so many others I have worked with over the years have shared that even decades later, a repair of some sort would make a significant difference in their healing.

It is never too late to sit down and write a letter or pick up the phone. Words such as, "You know I have been thinking about..." or... "I'm sorry, I don't think I handled that very well..." could forever change the emotional landscape of someone's life. When we know better, we do better. It doesn't matter if it was twenty years ago or yesterday. It is never too late to do our part to repair.

There is a powerful scene in the movie Million Dollar Baby where Clint Eastwood consistently sends letters to his estranged daughter only to receive them back unopened. As he receives the unopened returned letters, he carefully files them away in shoeboxes in his closet. The implication is that one day if his daughter ever showed up and said, "You never loved me," he would be able to not only tell her he'd always loved her but also go to the boxes and show her just how much she had always been on his mind.

When I am working with people who are estranged from their loved ones and they tell me, "I am really sorry it all blew up, but what can I do—they won't talk to me."—I share with them this story from Million Dollar Baby. Repair anyway. Show up anyway. Yes, you need to respect your loved one's position of not wanting to hear from you while keeping that space alive and open for when and if they change their mind, making sure your apology has been known. Taking ownership of our part of the rupture, even when not acknowledged by our loved ones, still provides us with a measure of healing and personal growth.

When I am working with couples who are constantly in conflict, the problem tends not to be their arguments or disagreements but with their process of repair. We can spend years and tons of money reviewing the minutiae of the day-to-day missteps, pull out the scorecards and play a giant game of tit-for-tat. Or we can begin to fill the well. To lean into reparation, to lean into positive action, to lean into meeting each other's needs. Too often couples present to therapy saying they want to improve their relationship and wonder why things aren't better after months of coming in and focusing on all that is wrong. We can water the weeds, or we can plant some flowers. We get to choose. We will screw up. As moms, dads, partners, friends, colleagues, bosses, family members—we are fallible and screwing up is inevitable. What sets us apart is how we repair.

Are there people in your life where a reparation is overdue? It's never too late. I have even helped people construct letters of apology and reparation to people who have passed away. Owning our mistakes and making reparations and amends is as much for our sense of self-worth as it is an act of generosity of spirit for our loved ones. So, don't worry about being perfect or beat yourself up over and over for how you have messed up. Turn your focus to how you are cleaning up. We can strive to never leave a scar, but if we do, and we will, strive to be the best damn plastic surgeon in town!

Step in It, Pick It Apart, Go Around—Your Choice

I was taught this gem early on in my career by a very respected colleague and not only have I used it with countless clients over the years, but it has been my guide through many sticky moments in life. While I have shifted around their words slightly, the sentiment remains the same. Imagine you are walking down the street. It is a beautiful crisp fall day. The sun is streaming, it's cool enough to wear a light jacket, kids are outside playing, and the air smells like leaves and apples. All is right in the world. Suddenly you come across a big giant pile of poop in the middle of your path. It's swarming with flies, has been smeared, and smells disgusting. What do you do?

Do you notice it, walk up to it, step in it, and then start cursing at it? Do you yell, *What the hell are you doing on my path?* Do you sit down across from it, staring at it, and wonder, *why me?* Do you grab a nearby stick and start picking it apart, thinking that perhaps if you could understand the content and texture of the poop, it might help you to realize why it was there, what purpose it holds, and what to do about it?

Or do you notice it, wince at the smell, and keep on walking? *Yep, a little turd in the punchbowl* or, in this case, *a little turd on your sidewalk, oh well.*

When I put it in the context of a pile of dog poop on your morning walk, it seems absurd that you would step in it, yell at it, sit down and cry, or start picking it apart. Yet this is what we tend to do with the piles of shit that land in our path all the time. *Why did that person cut me off in traffic? Why was that clerk at the store so rude? Why did my neighbor not wave at me? Why didn't that person hold the elevator? Why hasn't my friend texted me right back? Why was my spouse grumpy this morning? Why was my boss being an ass clown today?*

The pile of poop on your path isn't personal. And guess what? Neither are most things that happen in our lives, even things that feel personal or directly affect us. But we feel justified in our feelings of hurt and anger. We look for evidence that we have been slighted or not treated well. And, as stated before, we tend to find what we are looking for.

As human beings, we are actually created with a negative confirmation bias. It's evolution. Back in the day, if you heard a thundering sound getting closer, you were much better off assuming it was a pack of wild animals rather than sitting at your campfire thinking *Hmmm, that sounds like 10,000 fluffy bunnies coming to join me for some campfire tunes.*

Our negative confirmation bias can and has kept us alive. While we still have this evolutionary knee-jerk reaction to assume the worst, it is no longer serving us. Sure, rely on it when you are in a dark alley, in a dangerous part of town, or in a situation that many would consider high risk. However, unfortunately, we tend to take most everyday things personally. We overthink the piles of poop we come across. We sit down with our microscopes and begin pulling them apart. We sit and stare at them, crying and screaming, making ourselves upset and wasting our time.

What do you do with the piles of poop that show up on your path? Next time slow down and remember... it's your choice. You could just choose to step around it, not take it personally, and move on with your life.

The Three Gs

Over the years I have worked with many people struggling with all sorts of addictions: drugs, alcohol, sex, porn, gaming, food, and relationships. I have also worked with hundreds of people who grappled to remain sane and grounded in their relationship with a loved one struggling with addiction. I would venture to say that one thing most of those loved ones had in common was getting snared by their own addiction to both the addict as well as their thinking and problem-solving about the addict in their lives. AA, NA, and Al-Anon all have amazing slogans to help serve as simple, direct prompts and reminders—the three Gs is one of them: Get off their back, get out of their way, and get on with your life.

You may have heard of the word codependent. While there are many wonderful books and hundreds of articles written about codependency, the most simple and direct way I can describe it is being a walking reaction to someone in your life. People who struggle with codependency often feel lost, confused, scared, frustrated, exhausted, isolated, angry, and anxious. They often become hyper-functioners who are wildly adept at anticipating problems, plugging holes, fixing, doing, questioning, preparing, and being on call 24/7 to mop up messes. Not only did I treat hundreds of folks wrestling with this, but I also understood it well because I was one of them. For years I thought if I just said it one more time, this time louder, this time standing on my head, they would hear me and change. For years I thought that it was caring to stick around when my limits had been crossed and my boundaries had been breached. *I mean, I was the healthy one. Right? I wasn't the one with the problem, so how could I leave? What if I left and things got worse?* So, I'd try harder, try longer, or try a new approach. And the longer I did this, several things happened. I began to feel like I was losing myself. I felt impotent and scared which only intensified my attempts at control. I began to break down physically and mentally. My mantra became "No good deed goes unpunished" and I began to slip down the rabbit hole toward martyrdom.

Somewhere along the way, I heard about the three Gs. I didn't like them. At all. Get off their back? *Who will hold them accountable if I do that?* Get out of their way? *Who will direct them towards more positive behaviors if I absent myself?* Get on with my life? *Easy for you to say! This is my life! If I step to the side everything will fall apart.* So, I dug in and tried harder. And I got more frustrated, angrier, more lost, and more burned out. I went back to the three Gs and decided I had nothing else to lose. I had tried everything else. I had always believed that martyrdom was narcissism dressed up in a nun's habit. Yet, over the years I had become the ultimate martyr.

It took a lot of soul-searching to finally admit that I was no longer on my own side of the street. Hell, by the time I woke up not only was I on their side of the street directing traffic, I was so far up their butt that when they itched, I scratched. The three Gs became a crucial slogan for my return to myself and a return to my own mental sanity and health. It took a long time for me to emotionally grasp that getting off their back wasn't abandonment, it was trust. Trust that this was their life, their time slot here on earth. Trust that they would and could make their own decisions. Trust something larger than myself. If what I had to offer could have really helped or saved them, it would have happened. But anything beyond expressing my concern, offering support, and establishing limits seemed to backfire. I came to realize that less is sometimes more. I learned that by getting out of their way, I was showing infinitely more trust in their capacity, as well as their right to make decisions for themselves than all my attempts at fixing, correcting, and controlling had ever communicated. I learned that they might have to hit rock bottom (many times) before they decided to shift. I came to grasp that they may never decide to make that shift and a devastating outcome was a possibility. This was, by far, the hardest thing to accept.

As I practiced the first two Gs—I then had to face the harsh reality of the third; I had to get back to my life. It's amazing how small my world had become and how far away from my own life experience I felt while winning the gold medal for being a controlling hole plugger. I had to work hard to re-establish friendships, tap back into my passion and my goals, and learn again how to take care of myself.

We don't implement the three Gs to shift the behavior of our loved ones. Many use this slogan and others as weapons instead of tools. This is YOUR tool, for YOUR life. A wonderful secondary gain might be that as you stop controlling, stop fixing, and stand down, your loved one takes up their life. But there is no guarantee. What is guaranteed is that if you work to implement the three Gs in your life you will start to reclaim yourself, act more consistently from a place of trust and acceptance rather than fear and doubt, and feel joy and contentment begin to fill the crevices made bare and dry from years of over functioning.

Are you a walking reaction to someone in your life? Are you over-functioning out of fear and doubt? Are you afraid to let go for fear that things will fall apart? Have your attempts at propping someone up worked? For them? For you? Do you find your mood state is directly tied to how well this person is showing up in their life? Do you find yourself hoping that if you can just say it one more time if you can just get their attention, get them to see it your way that things will be okay? Are you feeling rageful, anxious, resentful, victimized, lost, and/or confused? It may be time to pull out the three Gs and begin to implement them. They may make you feel selfish or afraid. Keep going. Find an accountability coach, a therapist, or someone who can help hold up the mirror and remind you that you are on your own path of recovery. Then… *Get on with your life!*

What's Lost, What's Left,
What's Possible?

I spent the first eight years of my career working with the dying and their loved ones. For two of those years, my work focused on working with children who were terminally ill and their family members. I may have learned more about life during those eight years than in all of my five decades combined.

While loss is an experience none of us can escape, I learned that suffering from loss is not inevitable. I remember one young woman that I worked with early on. She had breast cancer that had metastasized and had less than six months to live. I would go by to visit, and I would help her write letters to her children so they would have her words on special days that she would never get to see—their birthdays, graduations, and weddings. What was lost was abundantly clear. Given the trajectory of her disease, she lost the protection of the cloak of ignorance most of us coast through life with, not knowing our potential expiration date. But for this young woman, she didn't get stuck on what was lost, she focused on what was left and what was possible. She conserved all her energy to be able to be out back with her kids as they played, being present at the dinner table, and helping with homework when she was strong enough. She used her days while they were at school considering what was possible. She might not be there in person to attend their graduations, proms, and wedding days but she would sit at the table and use every last ounce of energy to write the letters. And when she could no longer write, she would close her eyes and very slowly and deliberately speak as I wrote the words on the cards for her children.

Another young person I took care of was a seventeen-year-old girl who was dying of cancer just two years after having lost her mom to the same type of cancer. What she lost was her chance to have a boyfriend, play on her high school sports teams, graduate, go off to college, or go to Broadway to see her favorite show. She'd never realize her dream of being a mom and bringing to her kids all the gifts she felt had been bestowed upon her before her mom had passed away. She also focused on what was left and what was possible. She asked me to help arrange to get her to a nearby restaurant to meet up with a few of her friends. Over her many months in and out of the hospital, she had missed several of their birthday parties. She asked me to help her buy a gift for each of them and then plan a dinner where she could present them, stating she wanted to feel like a normal kid for just a few hours. I was stunned. She was dying and yet she wanted to make sure her friends felt celebrated and honored. She gave them more than a gift of cool bath bombs and make-up kits that day. She modeled for them and for me true grace and the possibility to continue to look for what is possible even in the throes of tragedy.

We will all face many types of losses in our lives. From friendships to jobs to homes to our youth to our health to our loved ones and ultimately to our own time here on earth. Loss is truly the great equalizer. One of my favorite quotes is, "Don't take life too seriously, you'll never get out of it alive." As Brené Brown says, "No one rides for free." Sometimes the cost of admission in life is wildly expensive as we face tragic circumstances that feel unjust and unending. Sometimes we get lucky and seem to skate through life without having too many dark nights of the soul. But every human being will experience loss of some sort. It can become too easy and also quite justified to get totally stuck on "What is lost?" However, if we can mentally go high and wide with our perspective rather than getting lost in the weeds, we just might be able to tap into "What is left?" and "What is possible?" and create something meaningful alongside our pain.

"My Team Is On the Floor."

- Coach Norman Dale
(from *Hoosiers*)

In the motion picture *Hoosiers*, Coach Norman Dale, a former college basketball coach, moves to a small Indiana town to coach a high school basketball team. He is not a local, and his presence and his coaching tactics are deemed suspect by the town at large. He has a small group of boys to begin with and a winning season does not appear to be at all on the horizon. He begins to teach the boys the fundamentals: passing, running plays, conditioning, and operating as a team, rather than five individuals. As the season begins to take shape and the boys start winning, the town shows up in droves to rally behind their boys, still uncertain of this stranger who has appeared in their town. During a game, one of his best players begins taking (and making) shots that Coach Dale has asked him not to take. As the young man makes the shot, ignoring his coach, Dale benches him. The crowd is not pleased. A few minutes later when another of his players fouls out and there is no choice but to put his player back in the game to have five players on the floor, the young man gets up to check into the game. Dale looks at him and says, "Where do you think you are going—sit down." The crowd is perplexed and angry.

The referees approached him with raised eyebrows and said, "Coach, you don't have five players on the court."

Dale looks at them and says, "My team is on the floor!" The crowd yells a series of loud "boos," throws things at him, and then launches a campaign to get him fired. But it was in that moment, "My team is on the floor!" that Coach Dale taught anyone who was really listening just who he was as a person and as a coach. He would rather lose a game than lose his integrity. He would rather face a mob of angry spectators while doing the right thing, than give in, simply to win in the moment.

If you haven't seen this movie, I would highly recommend it.

It took me a few times watching this movie and a bit of age and maturity on my part to truly understand how profound an act it was for Coach Dale to make that decision. How often in life do we cut corners, give in, and act slightly out of our values and integrity to win the battle of the moment? It is so hard to stand our ground and hold our heads high while being mocked and judged, with figurative bottles thrown at our heads while we seek security and peace in our decision to be true to ourselves.

I see this with parents who don't follow through with their children. They don't hold the limit; they don't follow through with the consequences. Why? Because it's easier not to. We can take a lesson from Coach Dale's example: Although he had to battle through the short-term resistance of his players and townspeople, in the end, he gained their respect.

Coach Dale was not there to make friends. He was there to coach. We are not here to be friends with and liked by our kids. We are here to guide and teach them. Their favor and appreciation for us will grow as we are kind, clear, and consistent. When things got rough, Coach Dale didn't scream back, didn't walk away feeling like a victim, didn't gloat or act in a demeaning and defensive manner. He didn't demand unreasonable things and he didn't bitch about how hard it was to be a coach. He simply coached.

I had this phrase painted on an old wooden plank in my clinical office. It reminded me and a few of my clients that doing the right thing is not always the easiest thing. Sometimes we have to be willing to go it alone for a bit to stand our ground. I often used this quote when working with parents who were struggling with parenting issues and found it to be quite helpful and relevant. It's hard to establish a consequence for bad behavior, poor grades, or a bad attitude. It's not easy listening to your kid cry as they miss a friend's birthday party, don't get to join their friends out on a Friday night, or sit in their room and read while the neighbor kids play football out in the street. But just like Coach Dale, if you can hold the line, you are playing the long game. Too often we give in and play the short game; a willingness to compromise our values when we encounter resistance. The problem with this is that it often results in simply just monkey barring it through life in a sloppy, impulsive, and reactive way. When we play the long game, maintain our values, and figuratively employ coach Dale's "pass four times before you shoot" dictum into our lives, we become that disciplined, steady presence that our team—be it our family, our workplace, or our friend group—can rely and depend on when the game is on the line. Our personal integrity is one of our most valuable assets and preserving it is completely within our control. It's a key ingredient in maintaining a balanced life.

Ubuntu... On Three!

In the spring of 2007, the roar of nearly 20,000 angry fans screaming "Fire Doc" filled the Garden. I didn't grow up in Boston, but I spent enough time there to know that you don't want to get between a Celtics fan and a losing season! In 2007, Coach Doc Rivers had done just that.

Months later, during pre-season training, Rivers introduced to his squad a new concept that he had been introduced to: *Ubuntu*. Ubuntu is an African word that loosely translates to "I am because we are." As Doc explored this philosophy that had been a rallying cry for unification in South Africa after Apartheid, it resonated so deeply that he brought it to his team during the 2008 pre-season and asked that they study it.

In August of 2023, Rolling Stone Culture Council contributor Chris Schembra wrote an article about the concept of Ubuntu. In it, he shared what Doc Rivers had said and what this philosophic concept meant to him: "I can't be all I can be unless you are all you can be. I can never be threatened by you because you're good because the better you are, the better I am." Read that again. And again. I did. Now imagine that becoming a guiding principle in your life with your partner, spouse, children, friends, colleagues, and teammates. Imagine what could happen.

Here's what happened to Doc and those 2008 Boston Celtics. They embraced the principle of Ubuntu fully. It became their team chant: "Ubuntu, on three!" Early in the 2008 season, Doc Rivers had to miss a game to return to Chicago after the death of his father; as the team won with a buzzer-beater, they met at mid-court to celebrate as a unified squad. As the players were interviewed after the game, Ubuntu was noted repeatedly. In June of that season, the Celtics went on to beat their rivals, the Los Angeles Lakers, to secure the NBA Championship title. The word is even printed on the side of their championship ring.

Ubuntu is about interconnectedness and interdependence. It is about trust, faith, and being a giver with a spirit of gracious receiving. It is the idea that the whole is greater than the sum of its parts. It is rolling up your sleeves and not only doing your part but also helping the people around you to be the best they can be. It is the essence of successful teamwork.

This construct is relevant not just on the court or the field but also at our dinner table and in our most intimate relationships, as we can choose to show up well and support our people in being their best selves.

Slow down and take inventory of where and with whom the spirit of Ubuntu exists in your life. If you can't seem to find it, cultivate it. It has to start somewhere, so if it is lacking in your life, let it begin with you. Good begets good, kindness begets kindness, and Ubuntu begets Ubuntu!

WAIT—Why Am I Talking?

Have you ever found yourself unable to stop trying to make your point? Have you ever felt an urgency to say something, say it again, and then email it, text it again, one more time, and then one last voice message for good measure? If so, this acronym may become your new best friend. I first heard the concept of WAIT working in the realm of addiction, specifically for folks navigating codependency issues. The compulsive need to keep talking, keep asking, keep checking, and keep pushing in an attempt to control the chaos that often exists in loving and/or living with a loved one with various struggles such as alcoholism and drug addiction is quite common. The compulsive NEED to keep talking, assessing, monitoring, teaching, begging, and proving your point over and over again can start to feel like its own addiction process.

For example, if I ask one of my clients who struggle with compulsive "fixing" to just say it or ask once and then leave it alone, they will often report back a level of angst, fear, or discomfort that they, "…just couldn't help myself and decided to text just one more time." That angst, fear, or discomfort is similar to the highly distressing pull a person feels when they are trying to reduce other compulsive behaviors such as binge eating, seeking constant reassurance in a relationship, or trying to reduce their screen time or time spent on video games. Our threat response system and our reward center have been hijacked. If we don't yell at them, beg them, set a new set of boundaries or ground rules, and tell them for the thousandth time, then how will they ever change? How will things ever be okay? *Maybe if I just say it one more time, this time with a bit more force or a bit more kindness or a bit more threat they will hear me.* Just stop!

WAIT can be a useful prompt and reminder for many of us fixers, hole pluggers, and helpers of the world. It isn't just for those in relationships with addicts. In fact, sometimes we are the actual addicts. Addicted to helping. Addicted to worrying. Addicted to serving as the *go-to* person. Addicted to controlling chaos. Addicted to problem-solving. Addicted to speaking long after our "project" has shut their ears and left the building.

People will often ask me, "So if I stop asking, talking, directing, or pushing nothing will change, and then what?" I will often ask them how the constant rhetoric is actually working out for them. Most will say they are frustrated, exhausted, disheartened, wildly anxious, and unhappy. So, I will often conduct an experiment with them. We start with one week of them using WAIT when they feel the urge to hammer-call, hammer-text, say it again, or drive home the point one last time. Most will come back and report that nothing really changed in the behavior of their loved one and that they felt initially more out of control and scared. However, if they continued employing the WAIT strategy, they often reported life started to feel a bit lighter, their mood improved, and they began to feel a bit more empowered.

We usually hammer-text, call too often, over-talk, and hyper-direct because we are afraid and feel out of control. This is an invitation to remember that if we are truly paying attention to our own side of the street, there is little energy left to be overly focused on the details of what our loved ones, friends, and employees are thinking and feeling or how they are behaving.

"But Jen, what about my children? I am supposed to use WAIT even with my kids?" If you are hammering and yammering and going in circles, then yes, give it a try. Make your expectations clear, make the consequences clear, be committed to following through with the consequences, and let things fall where they will. You will be surprised how much more effective this approach can be rather than telling them for the "umpteenth" time (not quite sure that is a true number, but my mom apparently did!).

So, next time we catch ourselves over-functioning, driving home a point that has been "driven home" a hundred times, asking for reassurance for the 20th time, or feeling compelled to "say it one more time"—if we pause, breathe, and ask ourselves *WHY AM I TALKING?* we may just find it to be a game-changer.

Two Ears, One Mouth

This simple yet profound fact was pointed out to me in the first year of my career. I recall the moment quite clearly. I didn't see it as poignant or important and actually felt a little criticized by a well-meaning and highly seasoned chaplain who I worked with at the hospice in Houston where I was cutting my teeth as a new grad. This chaplain had not meant it as a dig or a criticism. He was appropriately interpreting my tendency to talk too much about things as an attempt to manage my anxiety and professional insecurity. I was too early in my career to recognize just how *okay* it was to not know things, especially things in the highly subjective and mystical nature of working with the dying. However, since that time, I have come to rely on his simple, direct message to remind myself that we were only given one mouth while we were awarded two ears, and perhaps the divine design was for us to listen twice as much as we speak.

How often do we find ourselves talking to alleviate anxiety or to control a situation? How often do we forego listening and possibly learning something new but instead plow ahead needing to be seen as smart and having something of importance to share? Have you ever been in a group or class and had your hand raised only to realize that you are so busy formulating your perfect comment that you have missed the last twenty minutes of the course or what others have shared?

It seems the world right now is not interested in discourse or the sharing of ideas. To do so, we would need to genuinely listen, be curious, and be humble enough to learn that maybe there is another opinion, something we haven't considered, or something we haven't understood.

Another thing I have learned in terms of building rapport and trust is that people are starving to be asked about themselves or to be held in mind. Do you genuinely ask, "How are you?" and then actually wait around for their response, whether it be "I'm fine." or "Not so good, you have a few minutes?" Or do you do what I often do, asking the question as a courtesy, but in no way, shape, or form expect (or often want) them to engage with me in some deep discussion.

If you pride yourself on operating with humility and being a life-long learner, then truly practice slowing down and listening. I remember once hearing the saying, "Opinions are like buttholes... everyone has one, and they often stink." Sorry, a bit of a gross analogy, but it's true. There are so many opinions swirling around now with the 24/7 news cycle and social media. Now everybody has a platform to spout their opinion, but is anyone really listening? We hear things in sound bites, often out of context and then immediately start speaking and generating commentary about what we have just heard.

Imagine if we all worked to listen twice as much as we spoke. Can you imagine the amount of conflict that would dissipate? When I have worked with couples over the years, it was quite clear that if I was dealing with a highly reactive, contentious couple who had weaponized words towards the other, what lay underneath was a deep desire to be heard and a great fear in feeling unheard and/or misunderstood.

Next time you find yourself going for the words to fight back, prove a point, show how smart you are, or stay in control of the dialogue, try to push the pause button and know that our divine design was to listen more than we speak. It's okay to listen, to take your time, and to stop filling the space with noise. It is often in the spaces in between, in the pauses, that great wisdom can be cultivated.

The Basketball Court

One of the best things to have ever happened to me was not making the team. It was 1982. It was seventh grade. "Basketball" up until that time in my life had consisted of playing HORSE in the driveway with my brothers. I was shy and hesitant. And I was short. Lord was I short! The day after the tryouts the coach gathered us in the gym. She announced the A team—my name wasn't called. No surprise there. The coach then announced the B team. Once again, my name wasn't called. I held back tears as I walked out to the car where my mom was waiting. "I didn't make it," I said as I toggled the volume button as "Jessie's Girl" filled our car.

It was the 80s; parents were not uber involved in their kids' lives, kids didn't start playing sports at the age of two, and there seemed to be much more tolerance for necessary consequences. I am sure my mom, being the practical 80s parent that she was, thought *well, she must not have been good enough*. She touched my knee, said she was sorry, and said, "There's always next year." I wanted to scream, but I bit my lip.

The next day I summoned the courage to walk into the coach's office. I thought I was going to throw up as Coach saw me, grabbed her whistle, and said, "Only have a minute, what's up?" I asked her what she felt I needed to do to make the team the following year. I'll never forget her words, "Swantakarski, I can never say that right. You are short, you aren't very fast, and you can't handle the ball. What can you do? Pick another sport."

Sometimes there are moments in life that define you. I didn't know it yet, but this was one of those moments. I went home and asked my mom to take me to Oshman's sporting goods store to buy some orange cones and a pair of practice blinders so that I couldn't look down and stare at the ball while I dribbled. I became the manager of the team but told no one that I was less than interested in refilling water bottles and keeping score. I wanted a front-row seat for the practices and drills so I could go home and replicate them in my driveway.

Our neighbors had two twin boys who played for the high school. I stuttered as I asked Vince and Derek to shoot with me and teach me how to dribble between my legs and behind my back. When no one was looking, I would hang from a bar in my junior high gym, hoping that if I could hang long enough, I could stretch myself to grow. I was twelve but could have passed for a nine-year-old. As summer approached, I had probably clocked well over five hundred hours in my driveway running suicides (line drills), dribbling with my blinders, shooting, shooting, and then, more shooting. We had a month before we left for our summer home on the East Coast, and I begged my mom to enroll me in a local boys' basketball day camp. She didn't think twice about it. Or at least she didn't show me she was thinking twice. I was the only girl among over forty boys. They beat the hell out of me over those two weeks. I would come home with a bloody nose and bruises from head to toe.

We left for Pennsylvania for the rest of the summer and every morning my mom would pack my lunch and a thermos of water and drive me down to the basketball court in our neighborhood. I would spend the day practicing and playing anyone who showed up. Boys, men, it didn't matter. Back in those days, it was rare for another girl to show up, but I didn't care. I wasn't there to make friends. I had my jam box with my mix tapes of motivation. My mom would show up in the afternoons with iced tea and extra snacks, and my little brother in tow and sit on the beach at the lake across from the court as we'd play horse and one-on-one.

As I started eighth grade, I told no one but my mom about my plan to try out for the team. When I changed my clothes and walked onto that court on the first day of tryouts, I will never forget Coach looking at me and shaking her head. I hadn't grown. Not in height, at least. But neither

Coach nor I was aware of just how much I had grown as a player. I found my rhythm as we showcased our ability to shoot, dribble and play three-on-three. Towards the end of the tryouts when we had to run suicides and the length of the court racing against our peers, I was less than a half step behind the top athlete in our school.

The next day as Coach announced the teams, she started with the B team. My name wasn't called. My heart lurched. She announced the A-team. And just when I felt she had called out the last name—she paused, looked at me, and pronounced my name. Correctly.

I made the A team as a point guard. I was one step closer to actualizing my dream—becoming Larry Bird! Ha! I watched the players whose names hadn't been called and I felt compelled to tell them my story, but I was still too shy. Just before she dismissed us, Coach said, "Now girls, be sure to get your mamas to get you into some comfortable sports bras. Except for you Swantkowski, your mom can get you some comfortable band-aids." The girls giggled, but I didn't miss a beat. Another one of those life moments. I had grown in more ways than just my basketball acumen. I had grown enough to understand that you don't always get what you want, people aren't always kind, and you can use anything— positive or negative—as motivation. Coach and her callous and careless words had offered me the gift of growing some pretty powerful scar tissue. Scar tissue, I've learned, is always much more resilient than the skin it has replaced.

I am also grateful that my mom stood to the side and let me be me. Let me get beat by those boys. Let me figure it out. She let me decide what my next step would be and then supported me fully in my decision. While I eventually grew in stature and loved every minute of playing ball over the next many years, I was certainly not good enough to consider a college career. But the basketball court had prepared me well for my role as a therapist. As folks often come to me feeling beat down, tired, and on the verge of giving up, the sentiment of these words from the great University of Tennessee coach, Pat Summit, help me to motivate my clients to take up their lives and actualize their greatness: "Here's how I am going to beat you. I am going to outwork you. That's it. That's all there is to it!"

A Joke Means Both People Should Be Laughing

In my work with couples, I cannot tell you the number of times when someone's feelings were hurt, their partner's response was, "I was just joking!" *I was joking when I made that dig about your cooking. I was joking when I said you are just like your mother. I was joking when I said I could see myself cheating with your cousin.* The thing about a joke? Both people should be laughing. While I am all for helping folks to have thicker skin and not take themselves so seriously, I am also all about people recognizing that jokes are meant to be funny—to both parties. *Just joking!* is not a hall pass for when we have pissed someone off or hurt their feelings. It's okay to state that we intended to joke, while we own that it didn't deliver the desired effect.

One couple that I worked with really struggled as they would both take potshots at each other's vulnerability and then use the *it was a joke* card. This adds insult to injury, and the person who is hurt is then often made to feel like a "sensitive snowflake." I put that in quotes because it was a direct quote from a person I was seeing in therapy to their partner. Add that plus other lovely additions such as *Lighten up, I'm joking* or *Jeez, can't you take a damn joke?* to the mix and things go from bad to worse. We need to know our audience. If we care about someone, then we should care enough to understand their Achilles' heel and work hard to not go after it. If someone we care about is sensitive about their looks or their weight, if we care, then we don't "joke" about it. If someone is a bit insecure, is it really funny to make an innuendo about another woman or man in an attempt to get a laugh? Again, this isn't to say that sometimes we really are joking, and it just hits wrong. It happens. While the title of this book still stands, and, indeed, we are not responsible for the existence or installation of their buttons (aka vulnerabilities and sensitivities) it is also a part of being in a loving relationship of any kind to get to know our loved one's buttons and do our very best not to push them. Sometimes, we are looking to get under someone's skin, toss a bit of our resentment out in the form of a joke, and often, there is a sliver of truth in every jest. We need to choose our words carefully. Our loved ones should feel the safest, the most secure, and the least threatened in our company. They should not have to worry about being jabbed and then made to feel crazy when the jab stings.

Just One More Stroke...

In the movie *Nyad*, Annette Bening and Jodie Foster capture the real-life story of Diana Nyad and her triumphant swim from Cuba to Key West, Florida at the age of sixty-four. Nyad's coach Bonnie, played by Foster in the film, knows that her best friend is delirious, exhausted, and almost ready to give up when she's just a few miles away from reaching her goal. A goal she had been chasing since the age of twenty-eight when she first attempted the swim and failed. Now at sixty-four, having nearly died on several failed attempts in the last few years, Bonnie stands on the side of the boat and tells her friend, "Just one more stroke" then, "Just one more." She is aware that if she tells her weary friend that it will be thousands of strokes to reach the shore, it will be unlikely she'll be able to summon the will to complete the swim. Bonnie breaks it down into simple, reachable goals. *Can you do one more stroke? Now, can you do one more?* This is how Nyad finds success and completes her life's dream—completing the 110-mile swim—a goal she could not reach in her late twenties in the prime of her athleticism, but now, at the age of sixty-four, she is able to complete it.

Earlier in the movie, Diana reveals why she now thinks it is possible to achieve this feat, believed to be humanly impossible. Her mind and her will. She states that in her twenties she had a powerful body, but now she has a powerful mind. She proves in the end that it is the combination of being strong in body and mind that is the winning combination.

But it was the wisdom of her coach who understood that when the walls are caving in and the floor is giving way, it is imperative to find small, reachable markers to hit over and over again, focusing only on the next step in front of you. Bonnie held Diana's larger vision in mind while she allowed her friend to simply take the next step—the next stroke—and then another.

In the world of addiction recovery, there is an adage for folks when they feel overwhelmed or lost in the process to *just do the next right thing.* If you think about never being able to have a drink for the rest of your life, you will feel overwhelmed. If you think about all of the events, all of the stressors, all of the parties that lay ahead in which you cannot drink your way into confidence, fun, or abandon, it can feel like an insurmountable task. So, just focus on the next right thing.

We are met with a million small tasks and thousands of crossroads in our daily lives. Get up or lay there? Get up.

Make the bed or leave it a mess? Make the bed. Eat breakfast or start your day on empty? Eat breakfast. Call your mom and dad or put it off? Call your mom and dad. Thank the person holding the door or ignore them? Thank them. Go to a meeting or head home to an empty home and grab a six-pack on the way? Get to a meeting. Exercise or eat a pizza? Exercise. Take the trash out or put it off until morning? Take out the trash. Ask for help or isolate and self-destruct? Ask for help. Say I love you or assume they know it? Say I love you.

Every day, we make thousands of small decisions that either get us to that shore in Key West, retreat to Cuba, or swim aimlessly, getting exhausted and delirious and ultimately going in circles. Where are you in your life?

We could all use a Bonnie in our lives. But more importantly, we need to remember Bonnie's words—just do the next right thing, just take one small step, one more stroke, then another, and then another, and eventually you will be shocked at what you can accomplish.

"How We Spend Our Days, Is How We Spend Our Lives..."

- Annie Dillard

I have referenced Stoicism a few times in this book. This philosophy of practical wisdom not only makes deep sense to me, but it has also saved my life a time or two—literally.

I don't know if the writer Annie Dillard practiced Stoic philosophy, but her sentiment captures it fully. From Seneca to Epictetus to Marcus Aurelius to current-day Stoic teacher Ryan Holiday; being aware of the fragility of life and making the most of each moment and each experience we are given is the key.

I used to dream about being a writer. At the age of forty, I was frustrated that I had not reached my goal. Frustrated that I hadn't published a book and secretly envious of those who had, I made all sorts of excuses for myself as well as projections onto others. *I don't have any contacts in the publishing world. I just don't have time. I have people that depend on me. They must have caught a lucky break. I could write something better than that if I tried.* I am embarrassed to admit that I chose to spend my days NOT becoming a writer. Then, I not only stood indignant and shocked that no one was beating down my door asking for my manuscript, but I silently sat in judgment toward those who had achieved success.

It is up to us to decide what we value and what matters in our lives. It is up to us to make that happen. No one is coming for us. No one is going to stand over us and make us eat right and exercise so that we can meet our health goals. No one is going to turn off the TV, shut down social media, and place a pen in our hands.

I mentioned previously that a few years ago I had a health crisis that abruptly interrupted my life and career. Unfortunately, I lost my way for several months and found myself brooding, frustrated, scared, and angry that this had happened to me. I felt I had worked hard at being a good person in my life and didn't deserve this unfortunate break. I spent far too many hours staring at walls, feeling sorry for myself, and dreaming of my old life. I fantasized about feeling strong in my mind and body again, rebuilding my career, and re-engaging in life. But as Annie Dillard states, the way I lived my days became the way I lived my life. Days spent navel-gazing, feeling victimized, feeling pity for my circumstances, and waiting to *feel* like going for a walk, reading, writing, and reaching out to friends and loved ones turned into an existence that was quite far from my hopes and dreams. Each day felt like Groundhog Day. I had good intentions, lots of talk about a disciplined schedule I would start next Monday, then the Monday after that, until I stopped believing my own bullshit. Then one day I was listening to Ryan Holiday's podcast, and he referenced the quote by Marcus Aurelius, "Waste no more time arguing what a good man should be. Be one." I realized the hard truth that mental, physical, and spiritual health were not going to come as a result of my talking about them. They weren't going to come knocking on my door looking for me and drag me off the couch to a healthier realm. I was going to have to save myself, step by step, day by day, to reach the life and the sense of self I envisioned. *

We don't have endless cognitive space or psychic energy. Remember, our give a f*cks are limited. Each step matters. Each task matters. The small things add up. This is true whether one's goal is to be a world-class athlete, earn a graduate degree, become more physically fit, or be a more patient and good-natured person. Start where you are. Start now. Don't waste time, otherwise, you may find that time will waste you.

Our lives are happening, we are becoming in each and every moment. What are you becoming?

*Author's Note: *So as not to minimize or be dismissive, I feel it is important for me to point out that there are phases and stages of illness and injury in which psychological and behavioral shifts may just simply not be possible. In fact, there are times when "pushing* out" may actually be deleterious and can lead to further complications in the healing process. Each person must judge for themselves where they are in their own healing journey.

The Deadliest Catch

One day years ago I was home sick from work. You know the kind of sickness where you are too weak to even pick up the remote and turn the channel? It was that sort of day. I was lying on the couch, in and out of a feverish doze, and noticed that there appeared to be a marathon of a show called *The Deadliest Catch* on the channel I had randomly picked much earlier that morning.

I had never seen this show before, let alone watched eleven back-to-back episodes. Dozing in and out and dazed and drenched in fever, I watched and watched as various *crews* took their boats out into the giant, freezing Bering Sea to catch crab. About eight hours in, I sat up on my couch and grabbed a notebook. I began to quickly and feverishly (literally) write out what felt profound to me. Looking back on it I can recall that suddenly Freud's theory of economics made sense to me on a deeper level. Unbeknownst to me in that feverish haze, I had stumbled upon my realization of what I now refer to as mentalomics—the economy of our minds (aka we don't have endless f*cks to give!).

I watched as these various crews would head out to sea for weeks at a time searching for a certain type of crab. They weren't looking for fish, lobster, or anything else—just crab and a particular size and species of crab to boot—not any crab would do. Their boats were rocked by the large waves; it was freezing cold and dangerous work. They would release enormous metal nets (crab pots) into the sea, mark them with giant buoys, and then return to them several hours later to pull in the pots and dump their catch onto the floorboard of the ship like a child dumping their Halloween bags excited to see their new treasures. But what fascinated me about this process was how efficient and effective they were at discerning what they should keep and what they should not. As they pulled these enormous pots onto their boats and dumped them out, men in bright yellow slickers began quickly sifting through the crab, fish, and sea crap, quickly getting rid of everything that did not fit their goal. Numerous crabs made it on board and were immediately tossed back into the sea as they were not the right type or size. The keepers were tossed into a hold below the deck and then off they went again in search of the next pot to pull.

As I watched I thought... *This is such a metaphor for our minds and living effectively.* These guys knew what they were looking for. They didn't stand around holding up a starfish, saying, "You aren't what I wanted; what are you doing on my boat? Why are you here? Why can't you be a crab?" All the begging in the world would never transform that starfish into a crab, they LET IT GO and moved on, continuing to focus on what would serve them.

So much of what we do in our lives is focused on the things that cross our paths, slide into our lanes, or land in our nets that are not good for us. These things deter and delay us from what *is* good for us or what will bring us closer to our goals. *Why did that person just cut me off in traffic? Why didn't my boss appreciate my extra effort? Why did I get sick or injured? Why was that person rude to me?*

So, imagine that fisherman standing on board the deck of his crab boat holding up a starfish, and instead of quickly tossing it overboard, recognizing it is not what he needs, he holds it up staring at it and thinking, *Why did you go into that pot? You aren't a crab.* As he paces back and forth wishing that starfish to be what he wants it to be, rather than what it is, he becomes more upset. It's a starfish, it will never be a crab. When he finally tosses it off the boat, he finds himself unable to let it go and is focused on feeling defeated, deflated, bothered, and thinking, "What the hell? That isn't how this is supposed to go—I am here to get crab."

We have to know our INTENTION. What are we looking for? Then, we can better recognize what we must let go. This doesn't mean that things can't land on our boats, which may be an unwelcome but pleasant surprise and better for us than our original goal. So, some flexibility and discernment are absolutely required. But my point is we often expend way too much energy asking, "Why me?" rather than "Why not me?" We tend to stare at and curse the sea crap instead of tossing it to the side and keep moving.

We have already established that we don't have endless psychic energy. We can't expect to live a calm, grounded, focused life and allow the turds in the road or the crap on our crab boats to stop us in our tracks. We can slow down, take a good look at it to see if there is some way it can serve us, and then make a quick and effective decision to accept it, let it go, or adapt and move in a slightly different direction.

When life changes in an unfortunate direction, we have to become skilled at looking at our new reality and make the necessary adaptations. We can't get bogged down and paralyzed in the analysis of it. Maintaining our sense of self and turning to our values and goals to guide us, we adapt to our new reality and LET GO of the *Why me?* mentality. *Why me?* is a waste of precious energy. Everything has a cost and turning inward and getting stuck staring at what feels like an unfair twist in our road is incredibly expensive. Similarly, when life changes in a positive way, we don't want to lose too much time stroking our own feathers. Why? Because one fundamental truth of mentalomics is the notion that *this too shall pass.* Just like the stock market can be up one month and take a drastic downturn the next, our lives are mostly outside of our control. Sometimes the high moments in our lives are a direct result of our hard work. Sometimes it's just dumb luck. Sometimes we bring our hardships on ourselves through bad habits of thought and behavior. Other times it's just the way the cards were dealt. Celebrate your wins, learn what needs to be learned from your losses, accept that you are not in full control of all the variables, and keep moving moment by moment with intention, attention, reflection, and gratitude. Rinse and repeat.

Stop staring at a starfish wishing it to be a crab. Clean out your nets and keep casting.

34 Door Number Three

By the time many of my clients come in to see me they are feeling highly anxious, sad, frustrated, or distressed in one or more areas of their life. In a state of high distress, it is common to move quickly into all or nothing and black and white thinking. When we are overwrought or scared, we tend to adopt an *either/or* mentality rather than a *this/and* way of seeing the world or our situation. The this/and mentality both relies on and is the product of psychological flexibility. Anxiety, depression, or heightened and dysregulated emotional states can reduce this flexibility as well as be a result of the reduction or absence of psychological flexibility.

So, what is psychological flexibility? It is the capacity to generate options and to approach the world with curiosity rather than pathological certainty. Those of us who can do psychological backbends tend to be good *mentalizers*. Meaning we can: 1) Be curious about our own emotional landscape while being simultaneously curious about the mind of someone else; 2) Be empathic while operating from a place of self-compassion; and 3) Grasp and allow for the space between where we end and someone else begins.

As anxiety and distressing mental states can evoke psychological rigidity, we are left feeling that we are without hope and cannot see all the options available to us. Options are as essential to us as the oxygen we breathe as we navigate the world. We are never without options, even in the most dire of circumstances. Viktor Frankl and James Stockdale who respectively navigated treacherous concentration camps and POW camp experiences, taught us about the most important option of them all—the capacity to choose their response to their circumstances. This is what kept them psychologically intact while so many of their comrades collapsed under the weight of the traumatic situation.

Most of us are not living in situations as dire as POW or concentration camps, yet often we feel trapped and lost. Let's use the example of Marsha who came to me because she was overwhelmed by her relationship with her adult son who struggled with addiction. Marsha had paid for numerous rehab programs and therapists. She had allowed her adult son to live with her when he would inevitably get kicked out of highly respected rehab facilities or sober living centers. When she first sat with me, she felt she only had two choices: let him come home again or completely estrange herself from him. She attended a support group and felt the message she was getting was to cut him off and have nothing to do with him. This didn't seem possible to her. She believed her only other option was to do what she had always done; let him come home where he would eat her food, not contribute in any way, often steal from her, throw fits of rage, and invite strange women over in the middle of the night. Marsha was distraught as she asked me for help in writing her "goodbye" letter to her son. I listened and watched as she agonized over this decision. I asked if she felt trapped. She nodded furiously with a look of *Are you seriously asking me that?*

She said, "I don't feel trapped. I am trapped. I can keep taking the hits from him or I can write him off. I didn't sign up for any of this, I just wanted to be his mom." I explained to Marsha that most things had more than two clicks on the dial. Rather than an on/off switch, I asked her to think about her situation and her potential response as a giant volume knob like on the old stereo receivers from the 1980s. We spoke about the fact that she seemed dead set on there only being two doors: door number one—invite him back in and take the abuse, and door number two—become estranged from him and write him off. I asked what might lie behind door number three.

As we slowed down to explore what other options might be viable, I could see that she was starting to calm down. Her brow became less furrowed and her whole body seemed less rigid. By the end of the third session, Marsha had realized that she could still have her dream of "being his mom" while also protecting herself. She drew a line in the sand and told her son that she was open to paying for one more treatment stay and gave him the choice of two options that she had fully researched. She explained to him that there would be no more staying at her home, but when he got out of treatment or if he chose not to go, she would match whatever monthly income he generated for two years to help him get on his feet. Her son was notorious for starting a small business, doing well, and then walking out. She explained that she would not be a cosigner on any future leases, car notes, or new business ventures. She told him that she would continue to pay for his cell phone as she wanted to do that for her own peace of mind to be able to reach him.

Over the next few months, her son did go to treatment and then came out and asked for money to start a new business. She held her ground and said no. He finally got a job at a restaurant and to her word, she matched what he brought in per month. Six months in he walked off his job, gambled the remaining money, and showed up at her doorstep. She told him she loved him and, once again, held her ground, not allowing him to move in with her. Over the next few months, she wept as her son moved from homeless shelter to homeless shelter. Despite the fear and the sadness she felt for him, she remained committed to the game plan that she had laid out for him. She answered his phone calls, reminded him of his worth and that he was loved, but refused to allow him back into her home.

About ten months after our first meeting Marsha came in with a wide smile across her face. Her son had met someone who volunteered at the homeless shelter and hired him to work for his furniture company. This man was years into his own recovery and told her son that if he showed up consistently for work for one month, he would agree to let him move into his garage apartment for a small fee. Marsha was hopeful.

For the next several days every time the phone would ring, Marsha would fear that it was her son saying he had relapsed or lost the job. But that call never came. Her son kept the job, moved into the garage apartment, and eventually began to attend AA meetings. Two and a half years into our work together Marsha came in and broke down weeping with tears of joy. Her son had called her and thanked her for holding her boundaries while not totally giving up on him. She told him about her realization and implementation of the concept of "the third door."

She was beside herself when a few months later her son stopped by with a cup of coffee for her and told her how he had used the idea of the "third door" with a sponsee he had begun working with in his AA program. Marsha and I discontinued our work when she moved to her dream retirement town, but every once in a while, I'll get a text or a message letting me know how well she is doing and how healthy her relationship with her son remains to this day.

So, the next time you feel stuck between a rock and a hard place try to slow down, catch your breath, and make some room for wisdom to show its hand as you remember the lives of Frankl and Stockdale and figure out what a possible third door might be for you.

The Lifeguard

When I was fifteen years old and spent my summers up at our lake house in Pennsylvania, my friend Kent signed me up to take a lifeguard training class without my knowledge. I was angry at him as I had not expressed any interest in wanting to be a lifeguard. Kent went on to fail lifeguard training when he elbowed the nose of the instructor during a drowning simulation. I, however, went on to complete the course and pass the exam on a fifty-seven-degree, rainy day right before we headed back to Texas for my junior year in high school. I am forever grateful as my five summers lifeguarding up in PA on the lake beaches and pool resort in our neighborhood were some of the best and craziest times of my life.

Twenty years later, my lifeguard training showed up and served me in an unexpected way. I was working with a woman who was feeling exasperated and emotionally drowning in her attempts to save her daughter from opiate addiction. I am always a sucker for analogies and metaphors (though I never know which one's which), and suddenly, images from my moments in that freezing pool on that rainy day decades earlier popped into my mind.

For those of you who have never been trained in how to save someone who is drowning, let me explain. Imagine you are walking around the pool deck swinging your trusty whistle, making eye contact with your partner who is on the lifeguard chair, silently collaborating on when to blow the whistle and call the infamous and hated "adult swim!" You look over and notice someone is struggling mightily in the deep end. You run over and realize that a larger, middle-aged man is thrashing wildly trying to get to the side but is going under. You dive in and swim over to him. Now here's the important and relevant part: you swim up until you are about a foot and a half away and just outside of his grasp. At this point, you pull back and make a breaststroke kick so that now you are vertical in the water with your feet leading the way. You then take your right hand (if you are right-handed) and grab his right wrist, twist him around pulling him towards you but facing away from you as you put him in a cross-chest carry and begin to swim him to shore.

So, why is this important? Notice that you get close, but before you get too close you stop, get your bearings, and reach out from a position and distance of helpful intent. It would seem intuitive to think that you would simply jump in, swim up to the person, grab them, and pull them to safety. However, if you do that—guess what happens the majority of the time? The thrashing, terrified person will naturally grab onto you—usually right around your neck—and then you are both going down.

This approach—developing a position of helpful intent—is exactly what I teach my clients as they face challenging situations with loved ones who are struggling mightily with anxiety, trauma, emotional dysregulation issues, addiction, or any other struggle that leaves someone desperate and frantic. Close enough and positioned properly to be able to offer support and aid, but not so close and unprepared that they put themselves at risk of being taken under as well. Just like I had to undergo training to properly save someone from drowning, we often need help and support to develop a helpful plan and strategy to implement and maintain that helpful maneuver and position. Don't just jump in headfirst seeking to rescue. Slow down, make your plan, and remember first and foremost, you have to stay afloat to have any chance at helping another from going under.

Conflict Versus Deficit

Often people reach out to me for consultation about challenging dynamics in either past or current relationships. After I allow enough time to hear the story, I try to discern
whether the discord in the relationship is due to a conflict or
a deficit. Let me explain through an example.

Linda came to see me as she was having a difficult time
with her sister-in-law. In learning a bit more, she revealed
that her sister-in-law (SIL) reminded her a lot of her mother.
She described her SIL and her mother as both being passive-
aggressive, *shit-stirrers*, and relatively uninterested and un-
supportive of her. In fact, for most of Linda's life, she had
struggled to come to grips with her mom's cutting remarks
and negativity. Over the years, she pulled away from her
mom, even trying to find a geographical solution by moving
the family across the country. I don't happen to believe in
geographical solutions and Linda's continued struggle with
"constantly feeling triggered by my mom" while living two

thousand miles away simply proves my point. Not only was she dealing with the lingering vestiges of the hurt she felt from her mother, but she also now faced a SIL living just a few moments away who exhibited many of the same behaviors. Linda described her sister-in-law as constantly drawing comparisons between herself and her kids with Linda and her family; expressing interest in Linda and her kids but only to gather data to ensure that Linda and her family weren't *pulling too far ahead* in the game of life. Linda described feeling angry and agitated a lot of the time. She often felt depleted and worn out by the energy spent dreading family events and working hard to draw imaginary fences around her and her family out of protection.

I realized that to help Linda navigate her relationship with her sister-in-law, we might have to start with the original model—Mom. I don't believe that we need to spend months or years digging up the past to make changes in the here and now, but sometimes it is useful to illustrate patterns of behavior and reactions. We spent a few sessions discussing her mom, and Linda broke down a few times, saying, "I can never seem to please her." And "She always seems to find something wrong with me or what I am doing." And "If she sees my picture on Facebook, I'll get a text message telling me it's time to dye my hair or that my daughter's outfit wasn't appropriate. She has time to judge me but when I call and need her, she always has an excuse." It was clear that Linda was very hurt and angry by her mom's behavior. It was also clear that she was taking it very personally. I then asked Linda if her mom behaved similarly towards other people in her life. As Linda thought about it, she realized that her mom was like this across the board. Growing up her mom would have best friends that would suddenly disappear and never come around again. She recalled her mother constantly on the phone with people complaining about everything; the PTA meeting, the way the teachers taught, her husband, and how ineffective the people were who bagged her groceries or the crew that did her landscaping.

I finally asked Linda, "Do you think your mom has a great deal of emotional warmth, curiosity, and interest in others and simply withheld it from you? Or do you think your mom doesn't have much to offer anyone?" Linda thought about it and came to the realization that it appeared her mom could only extend support and kindness for so long with someone new before she resorted to her judgment and negativity. Linda and I discussed how we can't offer something we don't have. If the well of love, warmth, compassion, support, and curiosity is dry, it doesn't matter who it is—there's nothing to give. This is a deficit and quite different from a conflict. A conflict is when there is plenty to give but something has occurred between people, or a group of people, and one individual has decided to purposefully not offer warmth, support, or curiosity due to some specific conflict or problem. A conflict has the potential for reparation.

If we determine that we are dealing with an individual who just doesn't have it to give, we can shift the narrative away from taking it as a personal attack or affront. This doesn't necessarily make all the hurt magically go away, but it can go a long way toward understanding that we can't expect to get blood from a rock. We can shift our expectations and move ourselves out of a personal, victimized stance.

In the case of Linda, she was also able to recognize that her SIL tended to only have superficial relationships with friends and was wildly insecure. While this knowledge didn't allow Linda to suddenly enjoy her time with her SIL, she was able to stop feeling persecuted and the urgent need to protect herself and her family. Seeing her SIL as coming from a deficit model, rightsized the situation. She was able to put her guard down and see the judgment, contempt, and passive-aggressive behavior as unpleasant fumes of an insecure and unhappy individual. Over time, Linda was able to feel a great deal of empathy towards both her mother and her SIL as she recognized the smoke and mirrors for what they were and chose not to take them personally.

Slowing down and looking at relational challenges in our lives through the framework of a conflict or deficit can be particularly useful. If it's a conflict, you can choose whether reparations are needed or wanted. If it's a deficit, we can stop taking it personally and shift our expectations to a more realistic stance. This is not to say that someone operating from a deficit can't change and grow. They absolutely can.

But remember, we have to stay on our side of the street. You can certainly say how you feel clearly and directly. But we can't force a person to look inside, notice the deficit, and do something about it. That's their side of the street. Stay on your own.

Anxiety is Not Necessarily a Problem... Until We Make It One!

Thirty years ago, when I began my career as a therapist, it was rare for people to talk about anxiety. Now, it doesn't matter where I am—the supermarket, a little league game, a party, or having a casual discussion with a neighbor—the word anxiety not only comes up OFTEN but is wildly misused. Anxiety isn't why you aren't getting on the elevator, boarding an airplane, going to the grocery store, not going to the dentist/doctor, or minimizing your time in crowds. It is the fear of anxiety that is keeping you from doing these things.

It is natural to feel anxious before giving a big speech, going on a big trip, going out to a social event where you don't know people, or feeling trapped in a tight setting. In fact, a little bit of anxiety often can lead to us performing well. We feel the adrenaline and we use that extra whoosh of energy to help us stay laser-focused or navigate a challenging situation. It is when that whoosh seems to come out of nowhere or sticks around longer than we would like that we begin to pay attention to and then fear this uncomfortable response.

Unfortunately, most of us are not taught that at times, nervous systems misfire. Hormones, stress, traumatic events, and sensory overload are just a few factors that can lead to a misfire in our threat response system. This can create a weird, disturbing, or racing thought process, a panic attack, a strange flutter in our hearts, a bout of dizziness, or a sense of being disconnected from ourselves or the world. There are hundreds of manifestations of anxious symptoms. It is the ultimate shapeshifter, which only leads to more confusion and fear. Most people will have some form of a panic attack in their lives. This does not mean that most people will develop an anxiety disorder, or more specifically, a panic disorder. Most people who have experienced a panic attack think, "Ugh, that was awful," and then it passes, and they move on. For some, however, they will have a panic attack, and ascribe a narrative to it such as, *oh my God, that was horrible, I don't want to ever feel that again. What caused that? It happened in the grocery store or while driving—better not do those things—I don't want to cause another one.* This is how anxiety (simple firing off of stress hormones—adrenaline and cortisol) moves into an anxiety *disorder*. Disorder is when the anxiety that we experience, in the form of thoughts, feelings, or sensations, affects our decision-making and behavior.

Let me give you another example: Jill has just given birth to her first baby. On her second week home from the delivery, while changing the baby's diaper, she has an image of her baby rolling off the counter and dying. It's not an image she wants to have but she soon gets busy with her task at hand and forgets all about it. The next day, when she is changing her baby's diaper, she has a thought: *what if I were to drop my baby on purpose?* Now the whoosh of fear comes in a bit stronger, and she starts to become afraid of this thought and image. As the days and weeks go on, she wakes up and thinks *I hope I don't think that thought again.* BOOM! The image pops back in, but this time, she thinks, *what if I hurt my child? Do I want to hurt my baby?* The more Jill starts to fear her thinking and worrying that something might be wrong with her, the more she is adding fear to fear and is, unbeknownst to her, keeping the thoughts and images stuck. As she worries about her competence as a mother and fears her own mind, she is adding adrenaline and cortisol to her already sensitized state, and the anxiety is growing. Had someone explained to Jill that most new mothers have some form of unwanted, intrusive thoughts or images about hurting their baby, she would have been more likely to simply shrug it off as a misfire of her threat response system. She would have understood that anxiety misfires when stress is high (new baby and hormonal disruption), and stakes are high (caring for a new baby). While she wouldn't have enjoyed the imagery of dropping or hurting her child, she could have simply left it alone and eventually, it would have left her alone.

Our threat response systems often tend to misfire in times of overwhelm or the opposite—times when we exist without a sense of purpose—in essence, a state of underwhelm. Since we are living in a time where people describe being more overwhelmed and underwhelmed than ever before, it makes sense that more misfires would be occurring. Unfortunately, alongside the rise in misfires, there has not been a rise in useful information about how to navigate these misfires. Thus, there has been a dramatic increase in what we call anxiety disorders. Again, anxiety disorders are a disruption in our lives usually via avoidance, rumination, or other compulsions that we implement in an attempt to ward off further distressing symptoms. Anxiety disorders are a product of the fearful stories we create about the uncomfortable cognitive, mental, physical, and emotional anxious symptoms. While it feels like anxiety disorders *happen* to us, we have a role in maintaining and strengthening their hold on us. This is not to say that this is your fault. There are certain biological, genetic, and learned tendencies that make some of us more susceptible to turning anxiety into an anxiety disorder. But alas, this is not a book about anxiety and anxiety disorders, so if you would like more information you can log onto my website at jenniferswanphd.com.

There is a lot of useful information now available to folks, however, one may have to sift through the rubbish to hit the gems. In the meantime, remember that anxious symptoms (stress responses) can show up appropriately (public speaking, big test, big game) or as misfires; while uncomfortable and distressing, they are not dangerous. The real danger comes when we create a story about the symptom and add in some form of, *I don't think I can handle this*. That is when anxiety has a strong chance of becoming stuck and/or growing, disrupting our lives, and hence becoming an anxiety disorder.

Expectation Versus Reality

"There is only a problem when there is a gap between expectation and reality." I used to hate this quote. Why? It was taped to the refrigerator in my childhood home growing up. As a surly teenager, my mom would often simply point to the fridge as I was sent to my room for any number of reasons. Of course, back then I would skulk up the stairs, plop myself down behind my door, pull at the carpet, quietly scream, and secretly flip my parents the bird. I would imagine ripping the quote off the fridge and burning it with my car lighter—the very car that had just been taken away from me as I smarted off or came home later than my curfew allowed. But dammit, if she wasn't right. Yep Mom, you heard me, you were right! Most problems exist because there is a gap between expectation and reality.

I have used this quote with my clients, and I am quite sure they must have wanted to dropkick me and flip me the bird a few times along the way. But try it out. Think of a problem you are having. It could be with your husband, wife, partner, child, school board, coach, colleague, or boss. Now consider: If your expectations of them or their expectations of you were being met, would there be an issue?

While sometimes having an issue or problem with someone is called for and necessary, let's take a look at my teenage years to illustrate the problem when expectations and reality are not aligned. My parents' expectation of me was that I would be home by midnight. I got home at 12:30. Their expectation did not meet my reality and there was a problem. As a result of that problem, there were consequences. Consequences are a necessary and integral part of life. Unfortunately, too often we don't want to deal with the issue or problem and keep moving the goalposts down the field. Why? Because it's not a great deal of fun enforcing consequences. Sometimes, a problem exists, and what needs to change is the reality, not the expectations. This is the case with my being a pain in the butt teenager. If something was going to get me back into my car and with my friends, it was going to be on me to change my reality to meet my parent's expectations and get home on time. Had I tried to convince my parents to alter their expectations (and Lord knows I tried), I would have been met with more frustration and more time away from what I wanted to be doing.

However, there are times when we need to shift our expectations. Maybe you have planned to move across the country to your dream home in the mountains and start a new chapter of your life. As you are finalizing your plans, you go to the doctor for what you think is a bad virus and find out you have cancer. It's survivable but will require surgery and chemotherapy. You are currently living near a reputable medical center, but your dream home is at least an hour's drive from any good medical care. You could try to fight or challenge your reality, stick your head in the sand, and pretend the cancer wasn't there. Unfortunately, more than likely you would just find yourself becoming increasingly angry and frustrated. Or you could look at your problem and shift your expectations. Instead of being able to reach your dream destination in a matter of weeks, you could work to widen that gate and create a mental plan and goal of being able to move in six months or a year. You might shift even wider and simply say "I don't know when or if I will get to do that. For now, I need to focus on my health."

Sometimes it isn't clear if we should be shifting expectations or altering reality. It was often this dilemma that brought so many couples to my door for clarity and help. "He won't ever clean up after himself, and the bathroom is filthy," or "She continues to show up late for everything, and it's driving me insane." Regardless of the issue, framing the problem in the context of expectation versus reality can be helpful. Having a neutral party to assist us in slowing things down and looking at viable options, be it shifting reality (changing behavior) or shifting expectations can often facilitate a solution.

Cleaning Out the Cupboard

Over the years, people often found their way to my clinical practice, describing how they felt lost, out of balance, or that life was living them. Feeling chewed up and spit out, they would call me feeling anxious, out of control, or depressed. They would describe feeling like they just couldn't keep up. They came to me looking for answers. While I definitely had some opinions and tools to offer, I had come to learn over the years practicing as a psychotherapist that my real job was to help clear away the cobwebs, slow things down, and re-engage their wise minds so they could find that answer for themselves. More often than not when the dust settled, we would find the core issue would have something to do with a resistance to reevaluate and make necessary shifts to continue to grow and develop. We are organic, dynamic beings where change is always occurring. Sometimes the tools, strategies, beliefs, and ways of being that had at one time been helpful, we now find are no longer serving us. Unfortunately, many require being hit over the head with a two-by-four by life before they are willing to make a necessary change.

Somewhere along the course of my career, I heard this story: A young woman wants to cook for her fiancée for the first time and has decided to cook one of her family's favorites—roast beef. She calls her mother for the recipe and Mom explains that first, she needs to trim at least two inches off each side of the roast. "Why?" the daughter asks.

Her mom responds, "I really don't know. It's always how we've done it, let me ask your grandma." So, the call is made to Grandma to ask why it's necessary to cut off at least two inches from each side of the roast.

Grandma says, "I don't know, that's just the way I was taught by Me-maw (her mom). Let me call and ask."

Me-maw, now ninety-seven years old, answers the phone. They ask her why she cut two inches off the sides of the roast. Me-maw says, "I only had one small pot; a whole roast wouldn't fit."

I loved this story because here were three generations of women continuing to do something simply because that is what they had been taught. What are we potentially carrying forward for years or even generations despite it no longer serving us because "Well, that's how it's always been done."

Here's an example from my clinical practice: I was working with a young woman in her mid-thirties who came to me feeling a lack of connection to herself and the world. She had an excellent job, two kids, a kind husband, and a lot of friends. She was the President of the PTA, in charge of fund-raising at the church, and a first responder in her community for any and all issues that came up. She spoke about feeling like she wanted to crawl under a rock or at least take a six-month vacation. She told me she felt like no matter what she did it was never enough. For as much as she gave, she felt there was always more being demanded, more needed, more she could and should be doing.

As we began to work on creating boundaries, she was quite resistant and often did not maintain them stating that she felt "selfish." One day she walked in and started to cry. She began to tell me about her grandparents coming over from a war-torn Eastern European country and working two jobs to make ends meet. They opened their home providing needed refuge for other immigrants starting life anew until they died early of heart disease and cancer. She went on to describe her parents as being pillars in the community and in the church, never turning anyone in need away. She told me she grew up in a home where the stray dogs and stray kids always seemed to congregate. Often my client would go without presents on Christmas or her birthday as the family focused on giving to those in need. My client had been raised and steeped in a tradition of altruism and doing for others. *Doing right by others* through acts of service had been the family mantra. None of this was necessarily a bad thing, not at all. However, I took a moment and shared with her the story of the roast beef.

The next day she called me and said, "This *doing right by others first and foremost* way of life worked for my grandparents and my mom and Dad. Hell, it worked for me for a long time. But I am suffering, my family is suffering, and I can't keep up. This recipe doesn't work for me. I have a different pot and I need to do things differently." She had fully grasped the meaning of the story. It wasn't an easy shift for my client. She was going up against the generational attributes and habits that defined for her *how to be* in this world. But over time, she began to realize that blindly doing what she had been taught without looking at the ever-changing needs of herself and that of her loved ones, the family mantra was no longer serving her and had, in fact, become problematic. Slowing down to revisit what is working and what is not is imperative to feeling that we are operating at an optimal level emotionally and in our tasks and roles. Does your recipe box need an overhaul?

Be the Narrator of Your Own Life

Ever feel like you've lost the plot? Pressure mounting from work, family, friends, and keeping up with a life that is increasingly speeding up, can leave us feeling frazzled, frustrated, frenetic and/or fatigued and hopeless. Often people find their way to my office when they are stuck racing on a hamster wheel from hell or, conversely, feel that they have been flung off the hamster wheel and are depleted, lost, and confused. Somewhere along the way, for many of us, we can find ourselves simply going through the motions often not recognizing when or how we stopped calling the shots in our own lives.

Of course, I am not advocating for living in a bubble, tucked safely away from any expectations. We have to work to have mutuality with our partners and spouses, to operate with flexibility in our relationships with friends and extended family, and to not begrudge the sacrifice we have signed on for as we choose to bring children into this world. However, the goal is to do this while simultaneously remaining true to our own needs, desires, and limits. This fine line can seem impossible to see much of the time, let alone walk. So, how do we do this?

Wisdom.

Many of the chapters in this book have to do with cultivating wisdom. Realizing that wisdom isn't something that finds us, and it isn't something we often find when we are going 100 mph. One of my favorite definitions of wisdom comes from the famous Serenity Prayer: "God grant me the serenity to accept the things I cannot change, the courage to change the things I can, and the *wisdom* to know the difference." We can remain the narrator of our lives by cultivating the wisdom to know the difference between what we are and what we are not in control of. When we can keep this in the front and center of our experience, we can make good choices about our time, our efforts, and how and where we put our precious and limited physical and mental energy.

Here's an example: Mike came in to do some work with me as he was starting to feel depressed and frustrated in his life and his drinking had started to become problematic. Mike was the CFO of a large Fortune 500 Company. He was unhappy with the direction his company had been heading for a few years. He had four kids, one of whom had significant special needs. His wife was frustrated with him for traveling so much for work and spending less time with the family, yet he felt financial pressure to keep up with her desire for all four kids to attend expensive private schools, take tennis, golf, and horseback riding lessons and to maintain their membership at an expensive country club. His mom and dad were living across the country and needed increasingly more assistance. He was close to his siblings but was frustrated that they didn't pull their weight with his parents despite living closer to them.

Mike wondered why he had worked so hard to put himself through an Ivy League college and business school only to feel "road hard and put up wet" in his life. He felt like the more money he made, the more money he needed. One day he came in and handed me a sticky note with $54,000 written on it. I asked him what this was. He started to laugh, then cry. When he could finally speak, he said "That's how much it costs to run our life. Each month! I couldn't jump off this miserable ride of a job if I wanted to. I'm trapped." He admitted to having fantasies of checking out. He said he was not actively suicidal, but that he often felt it would be better if he wasn't here. "I am actually worth more dead than alive. She would have all the money she would need to keep living that life. I'm never around anyway. I spend more time in the air than on the ground, it seems. My phone literally never stops. Ever."

After we made a plan and a commitment that he would remain vertical and breathing long enough to see if we could make some changes, the real work began. It started with simply slowing down and beginning to challenge what was in his control to change, and what was not. He admitted that he felt he had lost any sense of *being in charge* of his life and often felt he was at the mercy of what his wife and the Board of Directors demanded.

I asked Mike, "Since a part of you has gotten to the point of wanting to check out and leave this life, would you be willing to see what's possible? It may not be comfortable, but I can assure you it will be better than the alternative." He nodded and said he was open.

Over the next year and a half, we slowly began to work from the inventory of what was in his control and what was not. We began to work on setting intentions that were in service of his values and goals. Mike was so overwhelmed at first that it was difficult for him to determine his own values and goals. As we started to explore them, they would quickly turn into what his boss, wife, parents, or siblings needed from him.

Over time we brought his wife into our work, and he admitted to her his level of hopelessness. While resistant at first and coming from her own place of fear of change, she simply pointed out how hard her life was rearing the children and trying to create a good life for them. Despite her initial resistance to seeing his despair, Mike began attending AA meetings. He gave up drinking and was shocked when his depression and frustration mounted instead of lessened. I continued to assure him that often things get worse before they get better. He continued in AA and joined a group of professional men who were working to be sober and increase a work-life balance. His wife was initially incredibly frustrated as he made his bi-monthly men's dinner meeting a priority. But he was steadfast and began to really understand that until he was back in the driver's seat of his own life, he was no good to anyone else.

Mike began getting up early to work out in his home gym. He would get up at 5 am as he had placed on his list of intentions to be the one to wake the kids and have breakfast with them every morning when he wasn't traveling for work. Mike slowly started to feel more in the driver's seat of his mental and physical health and began to feel better about his role as a dad.

With his marriage still quite strained, he put "focus on my marriage" at the top of his intentions and committed himself to telling his wife every day that he loved her, planning a date night once a month, and committing to two family vacations a year. His wife began to join us in our sessions once a month, and it was clear that she was feeling better about the marriage. She even hired her own life coach to begin to work on herself. They collaborated with a financial planner to look at their expenses and make necessary changes.

Mike asked if I would help mediate a call with his siblings regarding his parents. Over the course of four phone calls a plan was devised that involved all five siblings to address the increasing needs of their parents.

The next thing Mike tackled was his work. He began to

set boundaries regarding the amount of travel and time away from home. He spoke to his Board of Directors and was honest about his need to be home more with his family and to be more available to help his wife, especially with the help of their special needs child who required 24/7 care. To his surprise, the Board told him they did not want to lose him and to come back to them with a plan of what he felt he needed.

Eighteen months after our work began, Mike walked in one day beaming. He had signed up to be an Assistant Coach for his seven-year-old son's baseball team and they had just made it to the playoffs. He had lost forty pounds and no longer appeared as though he was carrying the weight of the world on his shoulders. He had reclaimed being the narrator of his own life. Narrating a story in which he was a good provider, an available husband, and a good role model of physical and mental health for his kids.

It's easy to land in a place where we have given up being the lead character in our lives, losing sight of the plot and unable to see the forest for the trees. Although not an easy or quick fix, slowing down to the speed of wisdom and living out our values and goals with daily intention can be a powerful intervention and can, as in Mike's case, allow us to come back to ourselves and to a life that feeds us rather than depletes us.

I've Stopped Self-Medicating... Now What?

Throughout much of my career, I have worked with adults who were interested in gaining control over their misuse of alcohol, drugs, spending, sex, relationships, or gambling. Often, clients would stop coming to therapy soon after they slowed down or became abstinent, convinced that life would automatically improve dramatically with this important change.

Unfortunately, it was all too common to get a call six to nine months out asking if they could come back in; confused and disillusioned that their anxiety was worse, their relationships still strained, and feeling overwhelmed as they attempted to face life and all its vicissitudes bareback.

Learning to live without alcohol, substances, or risky behavior to escape, curb one's anxiety, and help numb or reduce distress can be extremely overwhelming. Navigating work stress and a new type of relationship with their partner, spouses, kids, colleagues, and extended family without their trusty friend lubricating the way can feel like Sisyphus pushing the boulder up the hill. Only to have to do it again… and again… and again!

What I have found most important for people in early recovery (the first several years of sobriety) is to have an accountability partner. Whether that is a coach, a therapist, or a sponsor, I have found that it's imperative to have someone to help remind you that life without your substance of choice or other addictive processes can be incredibly challenging. For recovery to be successful we often have to build a new relationship with our minds and bodies. Knowing how to build that new relationship can be confusing and the effort can be daunting. Learning how to discern between the "noise" in your head versus the thoughts and ideas you should be listening to is key. The commitment to learning or re-learning skills such as tolerating frustration, regulating emotion, knowing your limits, and mentalizing in relationships can be highly predictive in terms of how successful one will be on their sobriety journey.

While not easy, giving up the substance or addictive process may, in fact, not be the hardest part. The more significant challenge for clients I've worked with is overcoming the loss of their "best friend." The friend that was there when life took them under, always ready and waiting to help them escape their pain and frustration. The whole world celebrates when someone walks away from their addiction, but often hasn't any understanding of the grief, fear, and sadness that is waiting on the other side. It is important to allow yourself to move fully through that process if you genuinely want to set it down and walk away. Many have heard of the term "dry drunk"—meaning, the person is no longer abusing alcohol, but their behaviors haven't changed. They still might be self-destructive or difficult to connect with healthfully in a relationship. This same phenomenon can be true of other substances, or for people that deal with things like gambling, sex, or relationship addiction. The substance or process of choice is often a red herring for a deeper issue. Addressing the red herring is imperative, but that alone may not be enough for real health to emerge. In addition to the underlying concern, issues of self-worth or self-esteem may be at play. Sometimes it is not being able to surrender or let go of a tendency towards perfection. Other times it may be that one simply hasn't developed the capability to modulate emotions or navigate their life with the temperance and practical wisdom that enable them to rely on an internal locus of control. As long as a locus of control remains outside of oneself, there is a considerable risk of relapse or simply substituting one addiction for another. If you are in the grips of an addictive process, slow down and think about who you can work with or turn to as you choose to take the high and hard road to prioritize your physical and mental health.

Like Nailing Jello to a Tree

Have you ever been in a relationship with someone who seems to move further away every time you move closer, all the while telling you that they desire to be close and in connection with you? Have you ever felt things were going well and then suddenly been met with intense insecurity, jealousy, and a desperate plea for reassurance that you would not leave them? Have you ever felt a deep connection with someone only to wake up and find they have fallen off the grid with no real explanation for their behavior? Conversely, do you feel that you can't seem to find the correct proximity and often miss the mark as you are accused of being too close or too far away? I have often described this dynamic as feeling like you are *nailing Jello to a tree*. The more you attempt to hit the nail squarely on the head, the more it slides through your fingers.

I can't say with certainty what creates this elusive, push-pull quality in folks, but I believe strongly that it is rooted in a person's overarching attachment style. There are four main attachment styles: secure attachment and three forms of insecure attachment, which are anxious-ambivalent, avoidant, and disorganized. Without diving deep into the profound work and theories of attachment, in short order, individuals who have a secure attachment tend to enjoy close, intimate relationships and are consistently and emotionally reliable in their adult relationships. Less securely attached individuals tend to struggle to obtain and sustain an intimate and trusting connection. For example, an individual who exhibits a more anxious-ambivalent form of attachment may present in a relationship with a deep need and hunger to have connection and attention coupled with potentially an even deeper fear of being abandoned or rejected. I feel folks in this category often evoke that sense of trying to nail Jello to a tree. They can vacillate from being connected and "all in" to being clingy and needing desperate reassurance, to distancing themselves dramatically to protect themselves from their deep-seated fear that they will be left. A sense of trust is deeply compromised in an insecurely attached individual. Many of these folks often have a fervent desire to have friends, have a partner, and show up well. Still, intimacy and a reliable connection are often overshadowed by their deep fear of feeling trapped, rejected, or abandoned. Thus, it can create a *slipping through-your-hands* phenomenon as we work to have a relationship with these folks. It can also generate a gaslighting and crazy-making effect as we grapple to find solid ground in their relationship. So, can someone like this change? My answer is absolutely.

However, change is only possible if that individual is willing and open to looking at their behavior, the mixed messages they are sending, and their desire to make a change. While many therapists tend to view attachment styles as fixed or permanent, I do not. I am not saying it is easy to begin to alter responses that may have been ingrained from an early age, but it is definitely possible. I used to think that one would have to do a "deep dive" and spend years working to understand why they show up the way they do in a relationship. While I think that can be interesting and helpful, I no longer maintain that stance. If someone can recognize their behavior patterns and desires to show up differently, it doesn't matter how entrenched or long-standing the pattern has existed; change is possible.

Unfortunately, most people I have worked with have been the ones trying to hammer the Jello to the tree. Frustrated and sad, they want their loved one to show up differently. If you are a fellow Jello pounder, you have to realize that your mistake is the incessant hammering. The more you hammer, the more elusive or dysregulated they can become. Your work is simple but not easy—drop the hammer. Be clear with your "Jello" that you will not keep begging them to show up in a particular way. Understand that their distrust is not because you are an untrustworthy person. Be clear that their coming closer, pulling away or demanding reassurance is problematic and not sustainable. And once you have been kind and clear in stating what is and what is not working, put the hammer down and stop trying to nail them down. Get off the roller-coaster and return to your side of the street. This does not mean that you have to give up on the relationship. It simply means that you cannot fill the hole of distrust that lives deep inside of them. That is their work to do. You can lovingly stand beside them if they choose to do this work. Couples work, alongside individual work, can sometimes be helpful as one or both people begin to look at attachment styles. However, sometimes, someone must do a piece of work independently, and we have to be willing to stand down and see if they are amenable to taking on that task. We also may have to be courageous enough to step away if they are not.

People can change. I believe that wholeheartedly. But we cannot change anyone. I could have been the best therapist in the world, seeing the problem clearly, but if the person in front of me didn't want it as bad as I did, nothing was going to happen. So, if you are on the crazy-making, whirlwind ride of hammering away and trying to nail Jello to a tree, please slow down, drop the hammer, and get back to your own side of the street. Once you are back in the land of what you can control (yourself and your response), you can decide if you want to speak the truth about the dynamic as you see it. It will be up to them if they choose to stop showing up as Jello. The only thing in your control is to stop chasing them down with a nail!

Like Washing Your Hair with Flypaper

Have you ever just not been able to let something go? A nagging thought, image, or fear that gets caught on the hamster wheel of your mind. Many of us take our minds way too seriously. I was one of those people as are many of the individuals I have worked with in my clinical practice over the years. We think that just because we have a particular thought or feeling, it is deserving of our attention. We are taught to "listen to our gut." But what if our gut has been co-opted by our sticky brain glitching out? We can find ourselves ruminating and rehashing. We can find ourselves researching, researching some more, evaluating, assessing, analyzing, and asking questions over and over like some sort of crazed prosecutor, until we are driving ourselves and the people around us crazy. It could be anything from *What if he doesn't love me as much as I love him?* to *What if I made a mistake?* to *What if I offended that person at a party?* to *What if something bad happens to someone that I love?* to *What if I lose my job?*

Honestly, it's endless what a sticky brain can latch onto. Real or imagined, past, present, or future. Scary or benign. It doesn't discriminate. So, what exactly do I mean by sticky mind? A sticky mind and anxious tendencies tend to co-exist together. One might even say, that having a sticky brain sets someone up to experience more disordered anxiety in their lives at some point.

When it comes to anxiety, we talk about the three Ps: predisposition, precipitating event, and perpetuating factors. It is believed that some people are predisposed to having a stickier brain than others. As kids, we may have been more suggestible and more highly affected by things we saw, heard, or imagined. Often there is someone in our extended family who also has a stickier mind. People with sticky brains are often highly intelligent and highly creative. We can also often be great problem solvers, fixers, doers, and hole pluggers. Our mind tends to be quite active, and thinking is one of our greatest assets until it becomes one of our biggest liabilities.

There is often, but not always, a precipitating event that may flip the active, highly engaged, albeit stickier, mind from a tool to a weapon. It could be a life stressor of some sort, hormonal imbalances, or simply feeling consumed by a fast-paced life. Regardless of the cause, when the sticky brain begins to take over and turns our attention and gaze inward to the point that we are missing out on real life in the here and now, things can get... well... STUCK. And this is when we must focus on the third "P"—what we are doing to perpetuate the cycle of sticky brain gone wild?

It is not uncommon in traditional talk therapy to get hung up on the first two Ps—our predisposition (in essence, nature) and the precipitating event (in essence, nurture). While potentially interesting and not altogether unhelpful, it is the focus on what we are doing or not doing to *perpetuate* being stuck in the loop of a sticky brain that is most effective when it comes to creating change. Once we determine that we tend to have a sticky brain and realize that certain circumstances, experiences, and stressors tend to push it into high gear, we can shift our focus to a new way of responding to our minds and not add gasoline to the proverbial fire.

Hank came into my office because he was struggling to let go of the fact that he felt his wife had cheated on him. His incessant questioning, checking, and asking for reassurance had brought his marriage to the brink of divorce and he entered our work in a desperate place. He had lost twenty pounds, wasn't sleeping, and described feeling tortured by his fear of her infidelity.

The endless mind chatter had begun after his wife had gone on a weekend girls' trip with four of her college friends to New York City. She hadn't called one night as promised and hadn't answered her phone when he had tried her. The next day when she called, she explained that she had developed a terrible migraine, had laid down for a nap in the late afternoon, and didn't wake up until the next morning. Her phone had died while she slept. She had been apologetic from the start, but according to Hank, "It was like a bomb went off in my head."

He described not sleeping at all the night she did not call. He didn't have any of her friends' cell numbers and spent the night pacing and contemplated getting on a plane to fly to NY from their home in LA, but he was responsible for their two young children. He recalled feeling further scared as he remembered stories of one of her college friends being a bit flirtatious and divorcing her first husband after having an affair. He told me he had never considered that his wife might cheat and described her as a loving, loyal wife.

It had been three months since the trip to NYC when he came to see me, and Hank found with each passing week he could not quiet the thought and images in his mind of his wife sleeping with another man. One night he had a dream about his wife and her ex-boyfriend having sex. Hank's jealousy raged and he found himself unable to concentrate at work. He would leave early or arrive home unexpectedly while the kids were in school, convinced he would find his wife in a compromising situation. He became irritable and agitated. He vacillated between desperate and asking for constant reassurance to being moody and doing things to make his wife jealous when they were out with friends. Hank, unable to quell the constant nagging images and thoughts, broke down and hired a private eye. The investigation yielded nothing, but a week later, Hank's wife found the business card of the PI that he inadvertently had left in the glove box of his car. His wife threatened to leave if he did not get some help. She agreed to couples therapy, but only after he had addressed his own issues with a therapist.

In getting to know Hank, I discovered that he had always had a highly active mind, imagination, and a tendency to ruminate or catastrophize. If his kids wandered out of his sight, he was quick to imagine something nefarious happening to them. When his elderly mother, who lived alone, didn't answer the phone, he imagined she had fallen in the shower, choked on food, or had let in a stranger. He described a time after being asked by his boss to go to lunch, spending hours in the bathroom with an upset stomach fearing he was about to be fired. The lunch ended up being a celebratory lunch offering Hank a promotion and a significant boost in salary. He also described constantly second-guessing the content and tone of his emails out of fear he would offend one of his colleagues. As I took a lengthy history regarding his propensity to jump to negative or catastrophic conclusions, Hank revealed that as a kid he feared his parents wouldn't return home from their date nights or his dad from business trips. He remembered fearing that they had been carjacked or killed in a car accident. The more I got to know Hank, the more I came to realize that his sticky brain had been with him his entire life. Hank also told me that both his mom and his aunt tended to be more anxious, ruminating about how the community perceived them and how they also struggled to let things go.

He described mounting stress at work, his mom recently becoming ill, and a slight increase in his consumption of alcohol in the weeks before his wife's NYC trip. All of this created a ripe environment for ruminating and catastrophizing as the idea of the love of his life cheating on him had been a thought and image too painful to bear. It took that small, ever-present sticky brain campfire and doused it with gasoline leading to a raging inferno. The feelings that accompanied the thoughts and images felt so real that Hank felt his *intuition* must be trying to tell him something. The more he tried to suppress the thoughts, the more he tried to reason with himself, the more he tried to get reassurance from his wife or the PI he hired, the more the fire raged. This is when I told him, "It's like trying to wash your hair with fly paper—the more you do it, the messier it becomes." Over time, Hank was able to recognize that it was his actions and behaviors, not his wife's, that were feeding the fire.

He accepted the first P—that he had most likely been predisposed to having an anxious sensitivity and sticky brain. He came to fully understand that his mind had always had the propensity to have a heightened, and often distorted, threat response leading him to imagine the worst outcome—often in quite vivid detail.

We also worked briefly on the second P—the precipitating event. He came to understand that the stress at work, his mom's illness, and increased use of alcohol, coupled with the intense fear stirred up by even the possibility that his wife could be unfaithful, had taken his normally sticky mind and set it ablaze.

We spoke about how a lack of certainty, a lack of control, and vulnerability are three main variables that can often lead to a heightened, and disordered anxious response. In addition, I taught Hank that the sticky brain and a distorted threat response did not respond to logic or reason, only behavior. Hank had to accept the reality that we can never really be certain if our spouses are faithful. In realizing this, he had a decision to make. He could continue down the path that would most undoubtedly lead to divorce, or he could drop the rope. He could make the conscious decision that his anxious mind was bluffing him, that his incessant attempts to understand what his brain kept showing him was like playing against a stacked deck, and that it was up to him to choose to stop playing the game. Since a sticky brain, and all the uncomfortable feelings it generates, are not responsive to logic, reason, or self-talk, Hank would have to act "as if" for a while and show his brain that he wasn't going to be bluffed. He would need to let the thoughts come while continuing to not entertain them. He would have to become a ninja of indifference to the noise in his head and call the bluff over and over again by remaining present in his life. Over the next six months, Hank became that ninja. He learned that not every thought that entered his mind was true, especially if it tended to come with a frantic or urgent whoosh of accompanied feeling.

While Hank will always have a mind that is stickier than some, he learned that his sticky mind didn't have to have him.

There is absolutely a time and place to rely on intuition and trust your gut. But if you grapple with a sticky mind or are operating from a place of urgency or anxiety, I think it's smart to pump the brakes and consider a new way before continuing to wash your hair with fly paper and wonder why things are such a mess.

Fix it, Flush It, Reset!

I was sitting at my twelve-year-old nephew's baseball game, and I watched as the shortstop was just slightly too short as he leaped to catch a line drive right over his head. Frustrated and beside himself as the dirt from the field rose around him, I heard one of the coaches in the dugout yell, "Flush it, kid. Now reset!"

Later in the game, as the other team's pitcher balked, enabling our runner on third to score, I heard their coach yell out, "It's okay, son. Fix it. And let it go!"

As sweat poured down my back, I smiled as I was reminded of why I love team sports. These twelve-year-olds were learning a key instruction to living a healthy life. Fix it if you can and reset. If you can't fix it, if there is no do-over, simply chalk it up to one of the millions of learning moments in our lives, then flush it and reset. I looked around at the group of parents that surrounded me in the stands and wondered how many of us felt we were able to master and implement these simple but profound words of wisdom in our own lives. Lord knows I try, but I certainly miss the mark a lot of the time! This message was further reinforced when I went home and watched a YouTube video of Jeff Callahan, author of the blog *Become More Compelling*, where he spoke about the value of this relational skill, *fix it, flush it, and forget it.*

Unfortunately, what I see frequently in my work with folks is the confusion between rumination and problem-solving. Problem-solving means there is a concrete issue and potentially at least one solution. There is a beginning, a middle, and an end to it. For example, using the little leaguers to make my point, one kid missed a ball that was hit over his head, and another made an error while on the pitcher's mound. While neither kid was happy with what occurred, problem-solving as an intervention was only reasonable for one of them. The shortstop couldn't will himself to be four inches taller. He could have sat there the rest of the game beating himself up for not being taller and nothing would ever have changed. The problem was not solvable. He had to flush it and reset. The pitcher, on the other hand, could slow down for a moment, remember the regulations governing pick-off moves to not incur an additional balk, fix what needed to be fixed, then reset and get back to pitching. Problem-solving for the pitcher makes sense.

Rumination has no beginning, middle, or end. It simply goes round and round, like a hamster on crack running on his wheel, going nowhere fast. The word rumination comes from the word ruminant, a subset of mammals (cattle, deer, sheep, etc.) that literally chew their cud, spit it up, and chew it some more. Yuck, but true. And that is what we are doing when we over-complicate our lives and don't use the flush it, fix it, and reset paradigm.

As we strive to be more emotionally effective in our lives, we have to slow down to check ourselves and evaluate how we expend our precious and limited psychic energy. Not only is ruminating and beating ourselves up over and over a waste of our time, it also negatively affects the people around us as well.

For example, one of my clients who struggled with over-thinking and rumination came in visibly upset after getting into a conflict with a new boyfriend. She was beating herself up that she hadn't been as attentive to him on a night out that had been planned for him to meet her friends. He was open with her later that same evening that it had hurt his feelings and she had apologized. Despite his immediate acceptance of her apology, my client continued to worry and beat herself up. Over the week that followed she had called him twice crying, continuing to apologize for her less than stellar behavior. By her third apology and obvious inability to let it go, he had told her he was getting frustrated and told her to knock it off. After we broke this down a bit, my client was able to recognize that she could fix it (apologize and not ignore him around her friends in the future), and then she had to flush in order to reset. By not flushing it, she kept circling the bowl, and her inability to let it go conveyed to her boyfriend that she didn't trust that he had truly accepted her apology. I said directly to my client, "So he first has to navigate you not being nice to him around your friends and now he has to navigate your ongoing emotional dysregulation because you feel badly—sounds like a lose-lose for him to me." He had trusted her enough to say how he felt, she had been strong enough to own it, offer an apology, and change her behavior in the future. Unfortunately, her inability to flush it kept her from being able to reset and re-engage, which only punished her boyfriend twice. What could have been a complete problem-solving cycle with a beginning, middle, and end became a ruminating hamster wheel from hell that was driving both of them crazy!

So, the next time you screw up, step on toes, or miss the mark remember it is up to you to determine if it is a solvable problem. If so, make amends or fix it and reset. If it is not a solvable problem, then do your best to not waste too much time in "shoulda, coulda, woulda" land and choose to flush so that you can reset and re-engage in life!

We Don't See the World as It Is...

In Chapter Two, I mentioned the quote by Anais Nin, "We don't see the world as it is, we see the world as we are." Let's take a closer look at how our perspective informs our thought process. Imagine you are visiting Seaside, Florida (my favorite place on Earth) and it's a beautiful early summer day. The waves are at a minimum making the ocean appear almost lake-like. It is a beautiful, zero humidity, eighty-two-degree day and the blue sky and the water appear as one. You are about fifty yards from shore on a floaty, drinking a cool strawberry margarita. As you look at the beach, there are lots of gorgeous people relaxing on their lounge chairs under their umbrellas. Someone is playing "Brown Eyed Girl" on their Bose speaker as children build sandcastles and toss a football. It is an amazing buffet for your senses, and you feel peace, gratitude, and a sense of connection with your fellow humans. Life is good. You are also having a bit of a delightful fantasy about one shapely stranger who has just entered the water in a bright green bathing suit. Suddenly out of the corner of your eye, you see what appears to be a large fin about ten feet from your raft. You sit up quickly to try to get a better look at what you have just seen. As you do, your drink spills slightly on your raft and down your leg. As you scan furiously, you see movement, but you can't make out exactly what it is. Then it's gone. You can't see anything, and the water around you returns to calm. You look towards the shore, and suddenly, it seems as if it is hundreds of yards away. You no longer notice the kids playing, the music, or the hot person in the green swimsuit. You don't feel connected to your fellow humans. The world hasn't changed, you have.

Our nervous systems are the power grid of our entire human experience. A nervous system that is in a state of safety tends to experience the world through a lens of connection and harmony. A nervous system that is either acutely or chronically sensitized tends to perceive the world as being scary, dark, creepy, and dangerous. The seascape, the music, and the attractive people haven't changed—our internal state of being colors our external perception. When the threat of a shark or other large sea creature enters the scene as a possibility, our threat response system activates. That threat response system—our limbic system—is not super smart, but it is incredibly loyal. It would rather be wrong one hundred times in case on the one hundred and first time it saves you. It doesn't care if you are happy or content in your life; its only job is to keep you alive and safe. How well would we have done as a species if we saw a shark approaching us but continued focusing on our margarita or the cutie playing volleyball on the beach? It's evolution. By design, when our physical senses detect a threat, our limbic system—evolved from primitive times when saber-tooth tigers and other predators threatened mankind—heightens our awareness and prepares our bodies for evasive or defensive action. Fortunately, in today's age, we no longer have to worry about saber-tooth tigers. Unfortunately, we still have this system that remains relatively primitive but loyal, and sometimes that system can misfire. Acute or chronic stress can move us into a fight-flight-freeze-fawn reaction in which teddy bears can become grizzly bears, and loving spouses, family members, and friends can be viewed as wildly disappointing. Just about anything can become suspect.

This isn't a chapter on how to navigate a sensitized nervous system (that's my next book!) but it is important to pump the brakes and check in with yourself. In that space between stimulus and response, before judgment, before you act, check in with yourself. Are you anxious, over-tired, over-stressed, agitated, or hormonal? Remember that your state drives your story. As you grasp this concept, you can then slow down, take a beat, let some time pass, and know that how you see things in the moment may not be an accurate representation of reality and you can adjust your actions accordingly.

Author's Note: *In the hundreds of times I have swum off the shores of Seaside, FL, I have never seen a fin or been scared off by a sea creature. But have I experienced feelings of peace, calm, and gratitude while taking in the pastel beauty? Yes, many, many times! I needed to qualify this point, as Seaside is my favorite place on earth, and I certainly didn't want it to be misperceived as an appropriate backdrop for a remake of Jaws!*

Generosity of Spirit

My Grandma taught me that there are two types of people in the world—givers and takers. She also told me that for every giver—there were at least ten takers. I grew up with parents who were both givers. They grew up poor but cultivated a life of emotional wealth. If they had it, then anyone in need around them had it. Similar to what I was referring to in my chapter on abundance and scarcity models, I was blessed to grow up in a home in which giving and viewing the world through the lens of abundance was a part of our family culture.

By mid-life, I had mastered the art of taking care of other people. My family, my clients, strangers... I was good at being a giver. It wasn't until my life took a strange and unexpected turn, that I realized that operating with a generosity of spirit was not just about plugging holes, showing up, and taking care of people and things. I learned that receiving gracefully was just as, if not more, important and that I was far less good at receiving.

When I entered into an unexpected health crisis, being a "giver" was just not possible for a while and I fell apart. *Who was I if I wasn't focused on being a good therapist and an involved aunt, sibling, daughter, and friend?* As painful as it was, in the absence of my being able to serve others for a period of time, I learned a great deal and did a deep personal dive into what it truly meant to operate from a spirit of generosity.

While my caregiving had a touch of altruism in it, I realized it had also served to provide me with a sense of being in control. I liked the feeling of being able to offer my help, support, and assistance. It gave me purpose and it fed my soul. But it also served as a protective shield. Extending the hand outward, I kept my vulnerability at bay. When the scales tipped and I found myself in a health crisis and somewhat debilitated, not being able to remain in that role of being a "giver" rocked my world. I now needed help—and lots of it. My family of givers stepped right up. I was so sick I had no choice but to accept their love and help. Unfortunately, in many of my relationships outside of my family, I isolated myself and hid away. People tried to reach out, they tried to understand—but I wasn't well versed on how to ask for or receive help. I felt out of control, vulnerable, and lost. Where was Brené Brown when I needed her!

Ironically, helping my clients be generous receivers has always been a large part of my work. Teaching them about being vulnerable, accepting assistance, and helping them to understand that allowing another person to offer you something was not being a "taker" — it was offering them the gift of being a "giver." We can see it repeatedly during natural or national disasters—hurricanes, floods, 9/11, war— when people come together, show up well, and want to help. Allowing that help and being a gracious receiver of that help is another way to give. But alas, the cobbler's kids often go shoeless, and I struggled to embody and implement the very sentiment I had helped so many of my clients create in their own lives.

I will forever be grateful for my breach in health as it allowed me to see that my generosity of spirit was out of balance and incomplete. It showed me first-hand how not accepting help for fear of being a burden was actually perceived by others as a rejection. Denying friends and acquaintances the ability to show up for me wasn't protecting them, it was protecting me. Protecting me from getting in touch with my own dependency and my own vulnerability.

The spirit of generosity is not one-sided. It is a spirit of mutuality and trust. It is a process of shared vulnerability. If you are one of those hole-plugging fixers and "givers" of the world, slow down and ask yourself how often you allow others to be their best selves in the service of you. Offering that space and role to truly show up for you may just be the best gift you can offer someone in your life.

Be Like Kelp

Have you ever been snorkeling and scuba diving and seen the gorgeous sea plants gracefully moving back and forth with the motion of the sea? Ever grabbed hold and tried to rip one of those suckers out of the sea floor? They won't budge.

I first heard this phrase a couple of decades ago when I was in a formal training program to get certified in Dialectical Behavioral Therapy. DBT is an approach that creates psychological resilience and flexibility by focusing on skills related to emotional regulation, mindfulness practice, interpersonal effectiveness, and tolerating distress and frustration. Kelp is a perfect metaphor for what it means to be psychologically grounded and resilient while also being flexible.

As the ocean churns in its constant motion, the kelp holds a stance of non-resistance and simply dances and bends. It doesn't bear down holding itself rigid and tight. Unlike an unyielding rock formation carved and whittled down by flowing water, kelp simply goes with the flow. However, to go with the flow and survive the constant movement of the sea, it has to be incredibly grounded. It is precisely because the kelp is so firmly and deeply rooted, that it can be so incredibly flexible and be in flow with an often-chaotic ocean scene.

This is true for us as humans as well. The more grounded and rooted we are in our core values and beliefs, the less rigid we tend to be. People who are deeply convicted are typically not screaming from the rooftops trying to convince others. They simply live out their conviction in their behaviors and actions. Individuals who feel secure in their skin are less vulnerable to the pressures of the world to fit in or comply. People who maintain their self-awareness and are grounded in their convictions know that we are not always in control and that's okay. They are secure enough to say, "I don't know," and typically don't feel compelled to walk around the world pontificating or pushing an agenda and illusion of pathological certainty.

Grounded and flexible. Rooted and in the flow. This is the way of kelp. It is also what it means to have mental resilience and psychological flexibility.

When You Find Yourself in a Hole, First... Stop Digging!

It sounds common sensical... yet I can't tell you the number of times I have witnessed my psychologically minded clients land in a hole and panic, thus losing sight of this simple yet profound truth. Truth be told, this has happened in my own life more times than I want to count. And I want to give credit to my dad's teaching for trying to instill this logic in us at an early age.

Unfortunately, it wasn't until deep into my adult years that the message took root!

We all fall into holes in our lives. Times where we have made a mistake and feel we can't find our way out or back. Times when we are overwhelmed, have procrastinated, or simply can't keep up and feel so far behind we just want to give up. Times in our relationship where we feel we have foregone our sense of personal power or integrity and feel weak and ashamed. The problem isn't that we have fallen, created, or found ourselves in a hole, the problem is that we tend to sit in the hole and either do nothing or become frantic and end up making the hole deeper.

Before we get to the simple logic of "stop digging," let me first explain something really important about holes. They lie! I used to talk with my clients about *the lie of the hole*. When we are feeling desperate, exhausted, hopeless, depleted, scared, out of control, and uncertain—our wise minds are not running the show. When our wise minds aren't running the show, who is? Typically, when we are in a hole it is our non-rational, emotional minds that are activated, and the volume is blasting. It is important to remember that state drives story. In the energy of the hole with the various highly charged emotions it is generating, we do not see the world as it is, but as we are. Thus, our thinking is going to become more negative, more rigid, and more catastrophic. *I'm screwed, this will never get better. I'm such a loser, this always happens to me. I don't deserve to be happy. I am a terrible person. The world is unfair and out to get me. I can't seem to get this right. I am a terrible parent/spouse/partner/friend/sibling. I guess I will always be alone. I don't know why I keep trying, it never works out anyway. Who cares? The cards are stacked against me. No one cares if I give up.*

So, our first step is to recognize we are in a hole. The second step is to remember that in a hole, we may not be in the best place to accurately assess ourselves, our circumstances, or the world around us. The third step is to see how we may be making things worse for ourselves by not slowing down and stopping our digging!

Michael came to see me as he was struggling in his relationship with his partner. He spoke about lengthy periods where he felt the connection was solid and they enjoyed each other's company. However, every few months they seemed to get in a fight over something relatively benign, blow it out of proportion, and it would lead to Michael saying he was ending the relationship. A cold war would then brew between them for a few weeks as they would separate. Ultimately, one or the other would reach out and a truce was called. This time, however, the cold war was not ending, and Michael found himself struggling to work or function well. He vacillated between feeling enraged and feeling desperate. As I learned a bit more about the dynamic, Michael owned that when things would begin to go off the rails, "It's like I enter this dark place. I reach this *burn it down* sort of mentality and usually put myself on a dating site and sometimes even meet a stranger out—just to prove I can." Michael admitted he didn't want his relationship to end but he knew the fights and the cold wars were taking their toll. He went on to say, "Once I am in that state, it's like a wire has been tripped and I can't walk it back. I say hurtful things and I go for the jugular. Eventually, I start to feel fear and terror and this terrible feeling of desperation, but it's like my pride gets in the way. One of us eventually caves, but maybe this time it's really over."

Michael and I began to see these episodes as "holes" and I described the various ways in which these holes could lie to us. He agreed and said, "Yes, for sure. When I am in that place, I try to convince myself that it's always been bad and always will be bad. I will twist things around, and I am convinced I am in an abusive relationship and that I need to get out. I can't remember any positive times or good things about my partner." He went on to describe that once out of the "hole" he could see all of the good qualities quite clearly.

Michael agreed that he needed to build some skills to help him either avoid going into a hole altogether or, at the very least, learn how to get himself out as quickly as possible. I had Michael write a letter to himself. It was a letter to Michael in a "hole" from Michael when things were stable. It was brief and he kept it in his notes on his phone. It simply read, *Michael, if you are reading this, you are back in a hole. Right now, you are in fight or flight mode and planning your escape. You are telling yourself that this relationship is a disaster and never was and never will be right for you. I am writing this just one week out of one of those dark moments. I love R, and in this current space, I can see all the good in the relationship. You aren't thinking or seeing things clearly. Stop digging. You guys always make up, so take the high road and call a truce. You don't have to drag this out or make it worse.*

Of course, there was additional work for Michael to do on his general patterns of hair-trigger reactivity and anxiety. But Michael credited this tool with shifting things with his partner for good. Over the next six months that we worked together, the cold wars between them had lessened in frequency and duration. Three months in they started working with a couple's therapist on communication skills and ended up marrying and moving overseas. Occasionally, I hear from him, and he always lets me know that he has continued to "stop digging."

The next time you find yourself in a dark place or a dark pattern, where light and hope seem dim and far away, be sure to slow down, evaluate the hole, assess the lie it may be telling you, and if you can't stop digging on your own, seek out help.

The Other Two Fs

Most of you have probably heard of the first two Fs of the threat response/trauma response cycle, fight and flight. But many know far less about the second two responses—the freeze and the fawn response. Before I break these four constructs down a bit more, let me talk about how and why these four F responses exist in the first place.

Simply put, we exist because we have a very loyal threat response system. Let me reiterate, a very loyal system. Notice I did NOT say an *emotionally intelligent* threat response system. Our limbic system, and most specifically our amygdala, makes up the most primitive aspect of our brain and central nervous system. It is not concerned about whether or not you are happy or enjoying your life. Its only concern is to keep you alive. Our amygdala and our threat response system are designed to detect threats, fire up the troops in the form of stress hormones, adrenaline (and eventually cortisol), and move us into some sort of immediate action. It's not interested in the details. It doesn't care about the narrative. That is for later and is the function of the more developed frontal cortex to sort out.

The freeze response is the third "F" of the threat response system. As it implies, in the face of perceived danger—the person goes still and becomes a bit of a deer caught in the headlights. It is my opinion that experiences of depersonalization, *I don't feel real* and derealization, *the world doesn't feel real* are manifestations of the freeze response. Woody Allen joked about it when he said that in the event of a war, he would be a hostage. I join Woody in that sentiment. Since I was a kid, I would simply go quiet and sit rigidly with eyes as big as saucers, holding my breath if I felt scared.

The fawn response is the lesser-known fourth "F" child of the threat response system. The fawning trauma response is seen in people who tend to people please, hole plug, placate, and tend to apologize or do anything to just make the conflict or scary situation stop. We often see the fawning response in teenagers as they try to fit into a group that is emotionally unhealthy for them. We also see this in folks in abusive situations as they tie themselves into pretzels and become human doormats, saying, or doing anything to try to get their aggressor to love them or stay. For years I worked with family members of folks with Borderline Personality Disorder, and I would watch them move into a fawning response as they tried to please their loved one or throw themselves under the bus just to keep the peace.

Our threat response system is incredibly important to our overall survival on this planet.

That said, when our nervous systems become taxed and overwhelmed due to acute or chronic stressors, our threat response system can begin to misfire. Remember, it's loyal. It would rather sound the alarm and send off a "whoosh" of adrenaline—just in case. When these misfires happen, we may feel a sense of doom, gloom, panic, dread, fear, or any number of strange and distressing sensations in our bodies. When we become afraid of these misfires, and code them as dangerous, we tend to automatically start to employ any or all of these four Fs with more frequency. As humans, we are not designed to be able to stay engaged and present in life while simultaneously operating in a fight, flight, freeze, or fawn response. Often, *evolution gone wild* wins out, and disordered anxiety takes center stage in our lives.

I could go on and on about what to do when this occurs, but it would require many more pages and much more detail and depth. For now, it's important that you understand that the four "Fs" are a normative response to an actual threat. However, if they show up at times when there is no real danger, it may be important to reach out to a therapist or coach. It is important to work with someone who can teach you how to speak the language of the limbic system. Someone who can work with you on developing behavior and mindset shifts to limit how often you are bluffed, minimize your inward focus on false alarms, and help you return fully to your life.

Waiting for Life to Begin

If I were forced to look at my three decades of working with people and name one of the most common struggles I have seen, it would be *waiting for life to begin.* From high-end executives to basement dwelling failure to launch twenty-somethings and all levels of education, all races, genders, ages, religions, and orientations, across the board, many people are living lives of quiet desperation as they lay in wait. Spoiler alert: There is no magic moment.

I think Nike had it right when they said, "Just do it!" So many of us, unfortunately, are waiting to feel motivated to start that new diet, workout routine, job search, search for a relationship, or make a necessary change. I have found that it most often works in reverse. You do it, and the feelings will follow. For some, the impasse comes due to perfectionism—*I don't know exactly what I want, so it's best to do nothing.* Or, *if I can't be perfect at it, I don't even want to try.* It is often in this category that I will also have the folks who can't start something until they have all the right equipment. I was one of those people. *I will start walking every day. BUT... I first need to have the exact right shoes, socks, shorts, and t-shirt and have mapped out the walking trail. Oh yeah, the weather needs to be not too hot, or too cold, and definitely not humid or rainy.* Ummm... yep, the walking is probably not going to happen.

I have had many clients over the years stuck in the same lie to themselves—*when this happens, then I can start. When my husband stops traveling so much, I can learn to cook. When my kids graduate, I can start to take care of myself. When my wife stops nagging me, I will come home earlier. When the summer comes, I'll start eating better. When the holidays are over, I'll start exercising.* It's a trap. Just do it. Avoidance and the compulsive making of plans that will start next week, next month, or at the first of the year, are time and soul suckers.

I was working with a middle-aged client who was profoundly stuck and struggling to take up her life. One day, I asked her how she felt about having potentially 180 months left on earth. Of course, I don't know if my client had another month or fifty years left to live, but I threw the number out anyway. I was honestly throwing spaghetti at a wall to see if anything would stick, and this one got her attention. For the first time, she spoke about being afraid that she would get to the end of her life and realize that she hadn't lived at all. She recognized the irony in that she had spent the last fifteen years after her last child left for college waiting for life to reveal itself to her and never stepping into life, thus ensuring her biggest fear would come true.

I asked her if she could fantasize about meeting someone towards the end of their life who she considered had actually "lived" and what that would look like. She went home and wrote out a description of an older woman who had traveled the world, was an avid reader, fluent in French, and had taken up swimming competitively at an older age. Her fantasy woman had friends of all ages, wrote children's books for fun, and went every Wednesday to shoot a gun at a shooting range. This woman woke up early, drank tea, did yoga, and had a meditation practice. She was active in the community and belonged to a book group where the members discussed literature while trying out new, exotic cocktails. Over the next few sessions, my client had fun developing her fantasy of a woman who, in her view, "had really lived." Of course, over time it became obvious to her that this woman was her. She was describing her own fantasy, and over time, we began to put things in place to begin to have her actualize what she had created.

At the beginning of our experiment, she would often come in and relay all the reasons why she couldn't get to the gym to swim, find the right book group to join, or start a daily yoga routine. Her motivation and desire to do much of anything lagged. However, over time and with the looming 180-month death clock in front of her, she kept going. She'd add in one activity and came to fully expect the resistance to rise up and meet her. She pushed through. Two years after beginning our work together, she was leading a book group, swimming and doing yoga daily, and volunteering at a homeless shelter. She had taken a bartending class, had gone to couples counseling, and had a pact with a couple of friends to take a five-day mystery trip twice a year in which only the friend making the plans knew the destination. She had stopped waiting for life to come in, wake her up, and reveal itself to her. She had created a life that she was proud to be living. Do you find yourself waiting for YOUR life to begin? It's already started, get busy living it!

Jane Goodall and Mentalization

I could write and speak about the importance of mentalization for hours and hours. Maybe a future book, who knows? For now, let me give you a brief introduction to the wildly important relational construct called mentalization and offer you a story that not only illustrates and embodies a true mentalizing capacity but when I heard it gave me goosebumps and changed my life.

Mentalization is not just the secret sauce for romantic partners. It is the key ingredient for any sort of relationship such as those between parents and children, family members, friends, work colleagues, and even more casual encounters.

Although the term didn't start to emerge in the psychological literature until the 1980s, its presence and importance are as old as man. It is the bedrock of all human relationships. It is a form of what we call social cognition. Perhaps we could see it as a form of emotional intelligence. We all do it at times, but some of us do it too much, not enough, or are not consistent in our use of this important construct. Roughly defined, mentalization is the capacity to hold in mind what you are thinking and feeling while simultaneously *being genuinely curious* about what the other person may be thinking or feeling. So, it is like the Brady Bunch of relational constructs—yours, mine, and ours. It is not a trait handed down genetically, it is molded and formed through healthy mirroring in our early years. This does not mean if we grow up in a non-mentalizing environment that we cannot learn this skill set, we can. But if we do grow up in a mentalizing environment it allows much more ease in our development of a healthy self and in having healthy relationships. I believe from the cradle to the grave we all have core needs of being seen, heard, held, valued, and understood. Being in a mentalizing relationship can offer fertile ground for these core needs to be honored and met.

Mentalization is the capacity and willingness to be curious, aware, and allowing of your own emotional state while *simultaneously* being aware of, curious, and allowing of the emotional state of your loved one/friend or colleague. Another quick way that it is often described is "Having a mind for your mind and that of the other." Sounds straightforward enough, right? Well, let's break this down a bit further.

Some of the main traits of mentalization are Flexibility, Compassion, Empathy, Interest, Curiosity, Interdependence, and Freedom. To be a bit more specific:

- Having compassion for yourself AND having empathy for others.

- Being reflective while also remaining open-minded about others.

- Being flexible in your thinking while remaining flexible and patient with others.

- Being genuinely curious about yourself and your loved one.

- Making space to *not know* how or what you are thinking and feeling in any given moment and being okay with that while you also allow your loved one to not know exactly what they might be feeling.

- Being able to exist in a space of interdependence.

- Recognizing that a relationship can only be as healthy as the environment between you and the other person.

- Having the capacity to recognize that people are not an appendage of us. They are free to say no, free to not know, and free to have a wide range of feelings, thoughts, and emotional experiences that might have nothing to do with us.

- Recognizing that we are not experts on anyone else. Thus, it is about staying away from statements such as "I *know* how you are feeling," "I *know* what you were thinking," "I *know* what he really meant," or "I *know* her better than she knows herself."

- Allowing room for us to surprise ourselves and for others to surprise us.

- Having the capacity to slow down to the speed of wisdom.

- Being responsive rather than reactive.

- Understanding that freedom exists in the space between stimulus and response.

- Allowing the space for people to make the right choices for themselves (even if they aren't the right choices for us).

Mentalizing is not:

- Making assumptions.

- Expecting people to know what we feel, think, or want (no matter how long we have been in a relationship with them).

- Overfunctioning because we feel we know best.

- Underfunctioning because we expect to be cared for.

- Being extremely self-focused.

- Being extremely focused on the other person.

- Posing what appears to be a question but there is really only one "acceptable" answer.

- Codependency in any form.

- Being reactionary.

- Using manipulative techniques such as stonewalling or gaslighting.

I regret not being able to give this concept its full due on the pages of this book, but it wouldn't have been complete without at least a reverential nod to this power punch of a skillset. I'll end by sharing a story I heard long before I was ever introduced to the concept of mentalization. As I said, on the night I heard this, I walked away with goosebumps, and my view on parenting and relationships in general was forever changed. Years later, when I stumbled upon the concept of mentalization, I now had a term to describe what I had learned from a random night long ago with Jane Goodall.

One year, my mom gave all the women in the family tickets to a Women's Speaker Series held in Houston. Jane Goodall was one of the speakers, and she was fascinating. Remember Jane Goodall? The scientist who studied chimpanzees by immersing herself in their environment at a time when the field was primarily male-dominated. At the end of her talk, there was a question-and-answer segment, and someone posed the question, "What made you believe you could do what you did? What made you Jane Goodall?" Jane didn't skip a beat and immediately launched into this story (it's been about 28 years since I heard this talk, so I'm paraphrasing at this point).

Jane had grown up in London and lived in a flat. No pets, no farms nearby, and little contact with animals in general. But she loved her books, and any books about animals were her favorite. There were some worms that lived in the flower box outside their flat and Jane loved these worms. One night, she went out and grabbed a few, and when her mom came to tuck her in, she found Jane dirty and snuggling with them. Jane's mom explained that they had their home and Jane had to respect that they needed to be in their own environment, then helped her clean up, clean the bed, and get back to sleep.

When Jane went to kindergarten, her mom had signed on as a chaperone as the class was taking a trip to a farm. Jane was beside herself with excitement, finally going to be able to see up close animals she had only seen in her beloved books. At the farm, Jane was fascinated with the cows, the sheep, and the horses, but then the farmer took them through the chicken coop and explained that a particular hen was getting ready to lay eggs. As they moved through the coop to wander through the rest of the farm, Jane held back and positioned herself in just the right place where she could watch this hen lay an egg. Jane was so enthralled that she didn't hear the calls for her that were becoming more anguished every few minutes. Jane's positioning had her out of eyesight and she was determined to watch the hen lay the egg. After almost an hour, with police and neighboring adults helping in the search and just moments away from the decision to search the nearby pond in case she had accidentally wandered off and fallen in—the hen laid an egg. Somehow, Jane was able to take the egg and walked out of the coop to find her mom. She recalled looking up and seeing what she said seemed like an army of angry giants noticing her, pointing, screaming, and running toward her.

She stood there holding the egg with the utmost of care, terrified of the mob rushing her way. When they got about twenty yards away, Jane's mom broke through the crowd, with a look of anguish on her face. Then Jane told the audience this, "As my mom got closer, she saw that I was holding the egg, and she plopped down in front of me and said 'Jane, tell me how the hen laid the egg." There wasn't a dry eye in the place when Jane was done with this story. We wanted Jane's mom to be our mom; we hoped we could be half as good with our own kids. Jane went on to say that she did, in fact, get in trouble later for her antics but that her mom took the one moment she had to be genuinely curious and offered that to her curious little girl. Jane's mom could have grabbed her, crying and emotional. She could have scolded her for causing such a scene. She could have been embarrassed for her daughter's antics; she could have been furious for Jane breaking away from the group—but there would be time for all that should it need to be expressed. However, there was only one moment for Jane's mom to put aside her upset, fear, hurt, embarrassment, and terror and be fully present and open to her daughter's experience. Jane said to the crowd, "And that is why I am Jane Goodall."

Let's strive to be like Jane's mom!

I May Have Pushed Your Buttons, But I Didn't Install Them!

I am not sure where I first heard this quote. Not only did it make me laugh, but it also resonated deeply. As someone who has certainly had their buttons pushed as well as someone who has done their fair share of inadvertently (or sometimes, purposefully) pushing buttons, I found it quite relevant in my personal journey as well as my work with others on personal accountability and responsibility.

As human beings, we all have our Achilles' heels, our vulnerabilities, and our wounds. I believe that a hallmark of being in a healthy, loving relationship, whether that be a loving friendship, romantic partnership, or with a family member means that as we have intimate knowledge of our loved one's "buttons," we actively seek not to push them. Yep, even when they are on your last nerve. That, in my opinion, is true love. *I could hurt you, but I choose not to.*

That being said, we will undoubtedly, at some point, hurt our loved ones. We will disappoint them, get things wrong, bumble, show up poorly, and step on their toes. We will stick our big fat fingers right into their wound, we will push their buttons. Why? Because we are human, and to be human is to be fallible. In my chapter on rupture and repair, I spoke about the importance of repairing as soon as we recognize our misstep or our loved one has said *ouch*. We need to curb the excuses and own our shit. Owning our stuff is not just about holding ourselves accountable when we hurt someone, it is also about recognizing that it is our responsibility to make sure that our baggage fits in the overhead compartment rather than expecting the world to not only make room for our baggage but anticipate and tolerate it fully.

We tend to only have a few handfuls (at most) of loving relationships. Loved ones who are committed to our well-being and who will not intentionally hurt us but will work with us on repairs should they be necessary. Outside of that small bubble is a vast and fast-paced world where no one is really paying that much attention. I happen to have a very positive view of the world and the people in it and believe that most people are not ill-intentioned. That said, they too will bumble, step on our toes, or push a finger in our wound. The key difference is they will not stop and work to repair with us. And if we walk through the world with the expectation that everyone will exhibit the same level of consideration as our loved ones, we will be wildly frustrated and disappointed.

Not everyone deserves to be privy to the stuff that makes us tick. Also, not everyone gives a rat's behind what makes us tick. Nor should they. For example, I don't expect the person changing the oil in my car or ringing me up at the grocery store to know that I don't like being called "ma'am" or that I find gum-smacking to be annoying. I don't expect the person in the car next to me to know that I have had a rough day and am racing home because a family member is ill. I don't expect that everyone is going to be just like me or have the same sensibilities and worldview that I do. That sounds wildly mature of me, right? Yep. But throw me in the middle of Houston traffic on a ninety-five-degree day after I have just had someone slowly BACK INTO a parking spot at the grocery store and watch how mature I am! However, it is during those times—times of stress and strain—that it's so important to remember that they may have pushed my buttons, but they didn't install them. Heat, traffic, people backing into parking spaces at a leisurely pace, grocery stores, and Jennifer do not go well together. It's a wicked combo. That isn't anyone else's fault. Nor is it their responsibility. That's mine to figure out.

As we move further into practicing personal accountability and responsibility we will naturally see more clearly where we end, and another begins. When we get and stay on our side of the street, we can increase our own sense of personal power as we stop projecting blame and realize that very few things are actually about us. We can allow others and ourselves to be fallible. We can choose to evoke a Frankl, an Aurelius, or a Stockdale and remember that the one thing that can never be taken from us is how we choose to respond to our buttons being pushed. We can turn back towards ourselves—our buttons, warts, vulnerabilities, and strengths—and realize that the buck starts and stops with us. This is when I believe we are truly free.

Jennifer Swantkowski

Jennifer Swantkowski is a mentor, coach, and consultant who works with clients worldwide, focusing on issues such as personal goals and accountability, anxiety, early recovery, and building effective and resilient relationships. Jennifer earned her master's degree in social work at the University of Houston and her doctorate at Smith College. During her career, she served as a clinician at two world-renowned psychiatric hospitals—the Austen Riggs Center in Stockbridge, MA, and The Menninger Clinic in Houston, Texas. She has also taught at the graduate level at Smith College, University of Houston, and Boston College. She resides in Houston, Texas.

To learn more about Jennifer, including her mentoring, coaching, consulting services, and contact information, please visit her website at www.jenniferswanphd.com.

www.ingramcontent.com/pod-product-compliance
Lightning Source LLC
Chambersburg PA
CBHW020233130626
46549CB00005B/1872